ALSO BY NATHAN McCALL

Makes Me Wanna Holler:
A Young Black Man in America

WHAT'S GOING ON

NATHAN McCALL

WHAT'S GOING ON

PERSONAL

ESSAYS

RANDOM HOUSE

NEW YORK

All rights reserved under International and Pan-American
Copyright Conventions. Published in the United States by Random
House, Inc., New York, and simultaneously in Canada by Random
House of Canada Limited, Toronto.
Grateful acknowledgment is made to the following for permission
to reprint previously published material:
NEUTRAL GRAY MUSIC: Excerpt from "Basketball" by Robert Ford,
Jimmy Bralower, Kurtis Blow, Shirley Walker, Full Force, J.B.
Moore & William Waring. Copyright © 1984 by Neutral Gray
Music/Fancy Footwork Music/Mokojumbi Music/Original JB
Music/Mofunk Music. All rights reserved. Used by permission.
THE NEW YORK TIMES: Excerpt from an article by Bob Herbert
from the April 18, 1997, issue of The New York Times. Copyright
© 1997 by The New York Times Company. Reprinted by
permission of The New York Times.
THE WASHINGTON POST: Excerpt from "Middle-Class Black Folks
of P & G County" by Kevin Merida (October 9, 1995). Copyright
© 1995 by The Washington Post. Reprinted by permission.

Library of Congress Cataloging-in-Publication Data
McCall, Nathan.
    What's going on: personal essays / Nathan McCall.
        p.   cm.
    Includes index.
    ISBN 0-679-45589-2
    1. United States—Race relations—Political aspects.
    2. Racism—Political aspects—United States.   3. Afro-
    Americans—Social conditions—1975–   I. Title.
    E185.86.M386   1997
    305.8'00973—dc21   97-18520

Random House website address:
http://www.randomhouse.com/
Printed in the United States of America on acid-free paper
9 8 7 6 5 4 3 2
First Edition

To my baby brother, Bryan
July 26, 1964–October 3, 1995

The time has come, God knows, for us to examine ourselves, but we can only do this if we are willing to free ourselves of the myth of America and try to find out what is really happening here.

—JAMES BALDWIN

CONTENTS

Contents

WHITE FEAR

INTRODUCTION

Several years ago, when I began working on my autobiography, *Makes Me Wanna Holler,* a friend who had already written two books of his own made an interesting prediction. "After this book is published," he said, "your life will never be the same." Of course I had no way of knowing what he meant. I couldn't have known. But in the years since then, I've come to see that his words were on the money. The 1994 publication of *Makes Me Wanna Holler* changed my life in ways, both good and bad, that I couldn't have imagined.

Mainly, the book tour and the lecture circuit that came after it took me all over the country to places I probably never would have visited otherwise. Along with the travels came the people. I met literally thousands of people, from Miami to L.A., from Montgomery to Denver. These were folks of practically every race and persuasion you can think of, and it often seemed that every one of them had something pressing that he or she wanted to discuss.

Some folks wanted to rap about various aspects of my life and the story I shared in the book about my experiences growing up as a young black man in America. Others had more personal, close-to-the-heart issues they yearned to address. Like the woman in Portland desperately attempting to save her fourteen-year-old grandson, a gangster wanna-be who had been hanging in the streets. She was trying to locate him because somebody had taken out a contract to have him killed. Then there was the woman in L.A. who said she'd once been gang-raped. She wanted to talk about men and the cultural conditioning that could lead them to commit such acts. And there was the East Indian guy in New Jersey trying to understand the hostility he often received from blacks. And, of course, there were many whites striving to comprehend the experience of being black and, in some related way, to understand themselves.

Often in my travels I encountered more people than I could handle. And I received more letters—gut-wrenching epistles that went on for pages and pages—than I could possibly answer.

At the same time, I saw and read about things going on around me every day that seemed to demand some kind of response. These were complex matters, social issues that were often connected in some way or another to the private pain expressed by many of the people I encountered. Particularly where black folks are concerned, there's so much unnecessary suffering being passed around, and much of it stems from America's unwillingness to confront its racial hang-ups.

What's been even more frustrating to watch over the past several years is the incompetence of white leadership. Rather than help alleviate some of the pain felt by the powerless, and rather than help solve some of the nation's social problems as they're supposedly hired to do, many white leaders have fanned the flames of racial antagonism. All for the sake of winning elections, they've gone all out to appease a childishly selfish white America, often at the expense of everybody else. These are the same politicians who promote harsh punishment for folks (most of whom are black) convicted of crack possession while allowing lighter sentences for people (mostly white) convicted of similar cocaine-related offenses. These are often the same politicians who talk tough about the need to crush gun violence and urban crime—a not-so-veiled reference to blacks—but who do none of that kind of grandstanding about gun fanatics, those crazy white men forming militias to overthrow the government.

But demagoguery is not confined to whites. During the recent outbreak of black church burnings across the nation, it was interesting to see how quickly some black leaders insisted that race was the sole motivation for the burnings, even as authorities turned up evidence that some of the fires were started by other blacks.

And those church burnings revealed another contradiction that sometimes hampers black progress. We almost always have a swift and powerful reaction to white injustice, but we seem to respond much more slowly when we're victimized by one another. No one can dispute the statistics of black men murdered by other black men, yet black communities have failed to respond accordingly. We haven't spoken out forcefully enough against those misguided blacks who help promote a violent mind-set that encourages young people to think that randomly taking someone else's life is somehow a heroic act.

These are just some of the things that have been on my mind as I've traveled about and talked with folks. Needless to say, I've been pissed off about one thing or another a good bit of the time, and when I get pissed off about something, I know it's time to write.

Eventually, it became obvious that I needed to do another book. In *Makes Me Wanna Holler* I related my experiences;

this time, I wanted to do a book that reflected my *perceptions* about some of the issues that divide people and keep us racially polarized. In an informal kind of way, I wanted to highlight the challenges of young black men and African Americans in general as we try to figure out how to fit in in this mixed-up country. I also wanted to examine why it is that so many white Americans seem to have a hard time respecting people who are different in color, culture, and values.

In doing this book, I shied away from issues-oriented essays. Instead, I used personal observations taken from experiences I've had while simply living and moving about in the nation, and especially in the D.C. area, where I live. In many ways, I believe those experiences are a microcosm of larger issues that people are wrestling with everywhere.

I also tapped the experiences of others. That required me to get out and use my reporting skills to weave into these pieces other people's observations about what's going on.

Although the topics here are varied, most of these chapters have one thing in common: They're related, either directly or indirectly, to race. That underscores my feeling that, as much as some people still like to downplay the role of race in this country, as much as they would prefer to emphasize how much "progress" we've made, race remains America's foremost preoccupation.

What follows here are pieces that represent a sampling of what I see going on all around us. It's not a particularly rosy picture. But then, our reality isn't a rosy one. These are my little truths, and if I may borrow a line from a review about a book written by E. Franklin Frazier, "A sad truth is better than a merry lie."

MIXED
MESSAGES

1

THE REVOLUTION IS ABOUT BASKETBALL

While riding through a wooded park in Arlington, Virginia—where the bike trails are longer and more scenic than those in my neighborhood—I came across a group of white boys shooting hoops on a crowded court. Curious to see if they shared the same electrified spirit that's standard at so many spots where black folks play, I stopped to watch. Except for the absence of trash-talking, funk-faking, signifying, profiling, and coast-to-coast monster slam dunks, the game was played with the same vigor as on any other court. One team, a group of dudes who appeared to be in serious basketball sync, ruled the court. They kicked *big* butt, sending one after another squad of pretenders to the sidelines in up-tempo games of "twenty-one."

I was about to leave midway through a game when a big luxury car cruised up, slowed down, and came to a stop. Inside were five black men who were apparently dropping in to check out the level of competition at that spot. After seeing the brothers, I sat tight, certain that some intriguing racial drama was about to unfold.

As the brothers popped from the car, their supercool demeanor revealed their self-assurance as clearly as the blue sky hanging overhead. Their smug expressions seemed to say, *We're* here now. The *real* ballin' is 'bout to start.

Almost instantly, the white spectators out there, who'd loudly cheered for their favorite teams before the bloods showed up, grew quiet, somber, as if a funeral procession were passing through the woods. They were afraid, I assumed, that there might be trouble.

Of course, the brothers knew they were being watched. (The white folks stared so hard they couldn't *help* but know.) Seemingly unconcerned, the bloods stepped to the sidelines and exchanged condescending smirks while they scoped the closing minutes of a lopsided game. Standing there, dressed in the finest brand-name tennis shoes and athletic gear, they appeared totally confident, cocky. Like maybe they'd taken in too many of those popular sneaker commercials that feed America's myths about their super ball-playing skills.

Perhaps they'd bought into that slick Reebok ad, the one where a brother, caught up in a fit of hoops bravado, boasts to the world, "This is *my* planet."

Or maybe they were inspired by the hip Foot Locker spot, in which a determined dude with a basketball spinning like a crystal on his gleaming bald head turns to Zen meditation to achieve white folks' idea of black men's greatest quest: defying gravity so we can dunk a goddamned basketball.

Possibly, the bloods saw Nike's revolution ad—the one that features several rising black NBA stars standing together, tall, lean, and solemn, while the voice-over informs us that "these are the men who will lead the revolution—because the revolution is about basketball."

When I was a teen, my buddies and I often listened to a popular political rap called "The Revolution Will Not Be Televised." Back then, that record filled us with the hope that one day we'd rise up from life's sewer and kick whitey's ass. Little did we know that our long-awaited revolution would one day be reduced to commercial breaks.

Now, seeing that Nike ad makes it all clear: *The revolution is about basketball. To bring on the revolution, brothers must leap in the air, not rise up in rebellion as we once believed.*

That's right. Stuff a ball in a hole, and all will be made right in our troubled black world.

The white champs playing in the park must have seen the commercials, too. The moment the blacks bopped onto the court to replace the losing team, the innocent game of b-ball ceased to be recreation alone. Right away, it was transformed into something else—something much larger than that. It took on the weight of a symbolic racial war, one that carried the strain of nearly four centuries of friction between American blacks and whites.

With few words exchanged between the teams, the black newcomers shunned their practice warm-ups and started the game. They began slowly, halfheartedly, as if they already knew how the thing would play out. They ignored defense; they trotted casually up and down the court and repeatedly tossed up bad shots—long, lethargic jumpers from three-point range. For the first few minutes, their cutesy fadeaways and show-off three-sixties bounced nonchalantly off the rim.

Meanwhile, the white boys ran on adrenaline, pumped by fear. They played a different, more determined game. From the jump, they hustled, defending strong against drives to the net, diving hard for loose balls, and passing to the open man for easy layups that caught the brothers off guard.

Seizing the chance to reverse the mental edge, the whites took an early lead. As they slowly began extending it toward twenty-one, concerned looks washed across the brothers' faces. The script wasn't unfolding for them in slow-motion splendor the way it did for the superbloods in those glossy sneaker ads. They huddled briefly, then nodded knowing nods that said, OK, *now it's time to start playin' ball. Let's take it to the rack.*

They picked up the pace, playing tougher defense, hustling for rebounds and using better shot selection than they'd used before. They dunked. They dived. They drove to the net. Clearly skilled, they were closing the gap toward the game's end, but it was too late. The whites had gained more confidence. They rallied desperately to maintain their early lead. Before long, it was apparent the brothers would lose.

As the whites crept toward the final score, one frustrated brother completely lost his cool. He called foul on a white boy who'd stuffed his shot. He insisted on taking possession of the ball out of bounds. When the white boy refuted the call, the brother, exasperated, shouted, "You hacked me, motherfucka!"

Actually, the guy hadn't fouled him. He'd blocked the brother's shot, pure and clean, and taken the ball downtown for an easy bucket. But the white boy conceded. He gave up the ball, then stole the inbounds pass and whipped it downcourt for another score.

Finally, the whites reached twenty-one. They milled around

the court, looking unsure about what to do next. You could see the triumph—and shock—in their eyes. I think they wanted to cheer. But the whites—about twenty-five spectators in all, including other teams and the champions' girlfriends—all lay low. They were afraid to celebrate for fear of being bum-rushed by frustrated black men who'd let their race down.

The bloods were pissed off for sure. But mostly, they were embarrassed that so many people—white people—had seen what went down. After all, those five brothers had come to invade the Man's concrete turf, to do their part for the revolution. Instead, they got slammed, *big-time,* at hoops—by *white* boys, at that.

The brothers lingered on the court momentarily in disbelief. Their pleading eyes hinted that they wanted to play another game—the best two out of three maybe—but there was no way they could ask without completely losing face. So they resigned themselves to the humiliating loss. They gathered their broken spirits, got in their car, and drove away, defeated in more ways than they probably realized.

After the brothers were gone, spectators, players—all the white folks out there—broke into a wild celebration, high-fiving one another as if they'd won the NBA finals or the NCAA. As far as they were concerned, they *had* won a championship. After all, they'd beaten a bunch of arrogant niggers at their own simple game.

Still unnoticed, sitting off to the side near the wooded trail, I watched the celebration from my bicycle perch, then quietly pedaled away, vaguely ticked off by what I'd seen. My feelings were marked by a gnawing ambivalence that I couldn't quite frame: I was glad, for their sake, that those conceited brothers had lost the match. At the same time, I was annoyed that the white boys had won.

Those conflicting emotions mirrored my mixed feelings about the game of basketball itself. I love the sport, but I hate the grotesque contradictions we Americans bring to the game.

For me, the players in that pickup contest acted out a drama that revealed just how much hoops reflects this country's fixation on color. Sports, for sure, is a metaphor for life. And in America, basketball is a metaphor for race.

From the get-go, both the black and the white competitors were driven by a crude assumption that's so firmly embedded in our psyches we don't even see it half the time: It's the deep-rooted belief that blacks are more gifted as athletes than whites but that God somehow shortchanged brothers on brains.

It was apparent from the start that the white boys believed the brothers were athletically superior to them. What annoyed me most was that the brothers seemed to believe it, too. Clearly, they showed up on that court *proudly* accepting the mythology that they were blessed with natural athletic skills. And because of that, they assumed they'd dust off the white boys and be on their way.

It's clear why brothers like them are so puffed up and proud of their proficiency at hoops. In a sense, they can rightfully claim basketball as their unquestioned domain. Since they got turned on to that white man's game, brothers have brought a poetic grace and style to basketball that's unmatched in any other sport. On sandlot courts or in pro arenas, African Americans do with hoops what Charlie Parker did with jazz—they highlight the beauty of improvisation. For brothers, basketball *is* jazz. It's their sweet obsession. It's ballet in sweat socks and tennis shoes.

Watching those bloods on the court that day also brought home the fact that many hoops-obsessed brothers seem to be missing a larger point: They think they're on top of the world because they can do a three-sixty or shatter a rim. But they haven't figured out how to transfer their ball-playing skills to the mental sphere. Their confidence and brilliant play mean that with similar time and devotion they could perform equivalent intellectual feats off the court. But they don't seem to get that; instead, they get hung up on their physical ability and play *right into* white folks' hands.

So many brothers get sucked into what seems like a basketball cult because they're conditioned to see themselves—and even to aspire to be seen—as athletic mules rather than as thinking men. Almost from the jump, they're encouraged—by the media, by whites, and even by the unwitting black athletes they admire most—to buy into images that lead to self-defeat.

To get a glimpse of how part of the psych-game is played, all you have to do is flick on the tube during basketball season, when the networks run a stream of glitzy ads that feed into a river of crippling myths. There's Michael Jordan, pimping his latest $125 Nikes by dunking a sky-high basket; there's Shaq O'Neal invading a graffiti-covered urban court to slam a ball before taking a Pepsi break; there's Jerry Stackhouse diving, like Superman, from a skyscraper; and there are others—an annoying assortment of glorified black hoops stars performing all kinds of superhuman b-ball feats.

The most powerfully persuasive ads tap into a deeply private emotional longing that some black men have: They'd probably never admit it, but they want desperately to win white America's approval and praise. Despite all their macho anti-white posturing, many brothers yearn to be seen as something other than the public monsters they're made out to be.

And advertisers gladly exploit that longing for white acceptance. Using everyday blacks and star athletes as props to sell hundred-dollar sneaks, admen allot black males a rare thirty seconds under the sun. Just think, we get full half-minute spots when we're transformed from dark villains into America's superheroes for a change. It's the only time they make us feel really special: *Like 40-ounce brew, brothers, these sneakers are made just for you.*

In one Nike ad, it's subtly suggested that brothers can become war heroes without even going off to combat. With a patriotic theme song playing in the background, several sweaty, sneaker-clad black men head boldly toward a basketball court. They're walking tall, in dramatic slow motion, like brave soldiers going onto a battlefield.

And who can question the influence of such ads? I recognized the power of the tube to alter reality years ago, when the government set out to erase the public's collective disgust with Vietnam. It flooded the TV airwaves with action-packed commercials designed to promote the military as a great career move. One ad had this catchy jingle, framed as a lofty manhood challenge: "Be all that you can be—in the Army."

In the years after that commercial aired, brothers every-where started signing up.

I became even more convinced about the commercial potency of the tube recently, while sitting in church. A little boy of about five sat near me, scrawling intently in a notepad. Curious to see what he had drawn, I leaned over. There it was: He'd sketched a near perfect version of the omnipresent Nike logo and scribbled the popular slogan, "Just do it."

Those sneaker ads—and all the messed-up mythology they perpetuate—get deep inside brothers' troubled heads. Mixed in with degrading real-life experiences that reinforce the ads' misleading themes, the mythology promotes the idea that black men are valued most when they're shooting hoops. It's no wonder they walk around believing that, as one blood's T-shirt declared, BASKETBALL IS LIFE! It's no wonder you hear so many folks humming the tune to the hoops theme song, popularized by the Penny Hardaway doll:

> They're playin' baaaasketttbaalll!
> We love that baa-sket-baall!
> They're playin' baaaasketttbaalll!
> We love that baa-sket-baall!

For whites, the glossy TV images of brothers as superathletes have a completely different effect. Their sense of supremacy is fed by seeing us portrayed as leaping monkeys, more closely related to beasts of the field than to human beings. Such notions are as old as the first European settlers on the continent; they're a convenient throwback to slavery times. They support the idea that, as someone once said, Abraham Lincoln freed the slaves so they could play basketball.

The reverence and awe that whites extend to brothers on the basketball court expose their hypocrisy in the worst ways. You see the duplicity in office settings, where black men are generally the last ones selected for crucial project teams yet are the first to be chosen during company picnics, when it's time to relax outdoors, drink some beer, and shoot some hoops. Yeah, when it's time to hawk ball, then *all* the white boys want a brother on their side.

You see it when watching those overhyped televised NBA games that come complete with clutch-shooting brothers and their adoring white fans. Looking into those screaming white folks' eyes, you can tell that they see no contradiction in worshiping a b-ball man like Michael Jordan while demonizing black men in general off the court.

The most appalling irony is this: Whites regard Jordan as America's premier race-neutral athlete, yet physically he embodies their most obscene fears: a six-foot-six *dark* black man with a shiny bald head. But Jordan's greatness at hoops somehow enables them to dismiss his darkness as a minor flaw, even as they allow their kids to bleat in cute commercials that they "wanna be like Mike."

And if the commercial admen and the whites aren't enough to daze young brothers' minds, the black players, whom they worship most, send equally confusing messages. There's something troubling about the way some black NBA stars naïvely accept white America's conditional love. There's something disturbing about those players who take the silver and run as far as they can from the very communities that nurtured them.

There's something annoying about a living legend like Jordan, who endorses products for Nike, Ball Park franks, Hanes, Gatorade, McDonald's, Wheaties, Renewal batteries, and Ray-O-Vac—but who refused to endorse a black man for the North Carolina Senate seat held by the racist Jesse Helms. In many ways, Jordan is a class act. But in others, well, I just don't know. . . .

To be fair, some ballplayers do give back to their communities, and their deeds often don't get noticed by the press. What we tend to see instead are the high-profile flashers, the ones who seem content to accept their appointed "place."

The blind eye that some pro players turn to white America's sham voids them as role models for the young bloods who look up to them. And so youngsters often don't get told—firsthand—that the revolution is *not* about basketball. Instead, they go on, inspired by the commercial hype. They grow up nursing juvenile dreams of being the next Jordan, Shaq, or Hardaway—rich, famous, and above all, loved.

You see them in backyards, on school grounds and city basketball courts, leaping, rising above the stars, descending to the court with flashy thunder-dunks. You see them out there, cocksure as hell, destined to learn the same hard lesson handed those brothers in that Arlington pickup match: that you can have all the natural skills in the world and still lose if you haven't mastered the mental game.

2

AIRING DIRTY LAUNDRY

Note: The author respectfully requests that white people abstain from reading this chapter. It contains material intended for black folks only and is meant as a personal discussion among us. In other words, this is family business, an in-house matter, a black-on-black concern not intended for consumption by the general public.

With the above disclaimer in place, never let it be said that yours truly aired black people's dirty laundry. Yours truly is fully aware—truly—that black people do *not* take kindly to such an offense. For some bloods, it's regarded as a crime worse than blasphemy. It's an unpardonable sin, an act of treason punishable by banishment from the race.

It seems that African-American writers, who sometimes publish works that reveal unpleasant truths about black life, run as great a risk as anybody of being charged with racial treason. For sure, if some "righteous" brothers and sisters had their way, black writers who air our dirty laundry would be taken to the chopping block and dealt with—righteously. They'd be hounded, like Salman Rushdie, the dude whose novel about Islam inspired Muslim fundamentalists to offer a hefty price for his balding scalp.

In the past few decades, a number of black writers have been subjected to less extreme, but more relentless, attacks by African Americans because of the notion that they violated some unwritten taboo about telling it like it is. In the 1970s, it was Michele Wallace, who wrote *Black Macho and the Myth of the Superwoman*. Then, Ntozake Shange caught hell for bringing us *For Colored Girls Who Have Considered Suicide/When the Rainbow Is Enuf*.

With all the debate generated by those controversial works, you'd think black folks would've worked through their misplaced anxieties by now. But clearly, that's not the case. After writing *Waiting to Exhale*, Terry McMillan got a dose of black rage from some brothers who questioned her devotion to the race. Black women worship Terry to the high heavens, but even today she has to tread lightly around these brothers. (One guy was so upset about her portrayal of black men that he went on *The Oprah Winfrey Show,* campaigning for blacks to boycott the movie version of the book.)

Few writers have aroused more fury than Alice Walker, whose 1982 book, *The Color Purple,* upset a whole lot of people. Although she wrote the novel more than a decade ago, Alice's name is still mud in many parts of the hood. Until things cool down, homegirl can forget about going down to the corner bar to get a taste. And if she happens to drop in at the Greasy Spoon for a pig-ear sandwich or collard greens, Alice had better order her food to go.

The truth is that black folks have spent a good part of the second half of this century dogging some of their best and most prolific writers when it comes to this business of exposing various aspects of black reality. They've harped on the issue so much that it may be taking a creative toll, affecting the literary judgment and decisions of black writers and forcing them to second-guess themselves.

Black writers really don't need a defense from me, mind you. Most of them would do just fine in a heads-up rumble. But for me, it's a matter of principle—free speech is free speech. It's also a practical concern: If critics will come strong after such luminaries as Alice Walker and Terry McMillan for airing black folks' dirty laundry, surely they'll come at the struggling wretches on the lower rungs of the black literary ladder, including me. And I hope my comrades in literature will have my back.

Blacks, of course, aren't the only people who are sensitive about how they're portrayed. Many Italians got pretty upset with Mario Puzo because they thought his classic book, *The Godfather,* and its movie version promoted stereotypes of them as a tribe of organized families made up of cold-blooded killers who would do anything to protect their criminal interests. Likewise, Philip Roth, particularly after he wrote *Portnoy's Complaint,* caught lots of flak from Jews, some of them saying that his novel about a neurotic Jewish man (who is obsessed with masturbation) is anti-Semitic.

The point is, every race has dirty laundry, and it seems that every group is sensitive about how it's depicted in literature and film. But this laundry thing has always been a fairly easy issue for me: The best way to get your laundry clean is to wash it. Then it should be hung out in the open—aired, so to speak—so it can flap in the wind and freshen, rejuvenate.

I would even say that our continued growth as a people depends largely on our ability to recognize the beauty of that cleansing process. And we must admit that at this stage of the game some of our stuff stinks *real* bad. Let's face it—at our best, we're as black and beautiful as beautiful gets. But at our worst, well, we be some ignorant niggas sometimes. Black-on-black crime, violence, pettiness, disregard for our children and elders, political apathy, disunity, and general chaos in black communities—you name it, we got it going on.

So I ask, Who more than our writers can expose the sometimes sick and trifling behaviors that impede our collective progress? Who else but black scribes can hold our dirt before us to be tossed into the wash?

As much as we're struggling to work through all the B.S. that white America heaps on us, you'd think we'd welcome the liberating insight that writers often bring to the table. But we often don't. We attack instead. We dust off the protest signs and take to the streets. We dog the messenger.

That knee-jerk response to unflattering portrayals of blacks is partly rooted in what I call the colored logic. The colored logic dictates that we black people always put on our best and most dignified, unified, and glorified face for white America, even if such an image misrepresents the truth. The colored logic argues that if we African Americans—er, colored people—air our dirty laundry, if we reveal the worst of what's going on among us, white folks will use that information to confirm the ugliest stereotypes they already hold.

Yours truly says, *Forget that.* And forget white America, too. In case you haven't noticed, some white people believe what they want to believe about black folks whether it's true or not. White people will continue believing what they want to believe about us. Some of them need to view us in a negative light in order to maintain a positive image of themselves. It's sick and it's sad, but it's also true.

Although *The Color Purple* and *Waiting to Exhale* were fiction, some whites (and even some blacks) elevated these works to the status of sociology; they treated them as documented proof of what one white writer described as a "festering animosity between black men and black women."

As I said, they believe what they want to believe, and some whites love to promote the notion that black men and black women don't get along. (It's funny, but the last I heard, white women weren't exactly turning somersaults over their relationships with white men. Books such as *The First Wives Club* reveal that white women have their share of complaints, too.)

As one writer who has been taking in all the shrillness in the portrayals of black folks in literature and film, I find it hard sometimes to be sympathetic to the fuss. I find the criticism particularly frustrating because I think I know something about writers' motivations. Basically, our goal is to get as close as we can to conveying our truth. We want to tell a good story. Selling books is important, too. But first and foremost, an author's aim is to get it right.

All this is not to suggest that I'm not sensitive to the delicacy involved in airing dirty laundry. I'm hip to the hurt blacks feel. I also understand how our laundry got so downright funky in the first place. It started long ago, when an entire race of people nearly had its identity stamped out and was left confused about who it was.

And it didn't help that in the years since then popular white culture has compounded the pain by portraying blacks in unflattering ways. In literature, film, and practically every other aspect of American culture, blacks have been mocked ruthlessly, from Amos and Andy and Buckwheat to J. J. Walker. White America has found fault—and laughter—in our every characteristic, from the width of our noses to the way we speak. They continue to ridicule blackness, and they seem to take a special delight in condemning black men.

Not surprisingly, this constant ridicule by whites has made black people hypersensitive to criticism of any kind from anybody—especially from their own people. White scorn has made blacks so edgy that they're distrustful, even of black writers who mean them no harm. We're a people who, in the words of Alice Walker, are "so wounded by betrayal, so hurt by misplacing their trust, that to offer us a gift of love is often to risk one's life, certainly one's name and reputation."

And who would know that better than Alice Walker? In *The Color Purple,* she wrote about four black women—Celie, Shug, Nettie, and Sofia—trying to survive in a male-dominated rural society. Within the confines of that world, some black men were tyrants, holding women hostage and even, God forbid, committing incest. *Lordy, Lordy,* the black people cried when the book was published. *What Alice Walker do that for?*

Black people, the critics charged, *do* not *commit incest.* The Color Purple *is white propaganda. That's why she won the Pulitzer Prize. That's why she made so much money from it. That's why they made it into a movie. Blah, blah, blah, blah . . .*

After publication of *The Color Purple,* black folks ate Alice Walker for lunch. They were still nibbling on chunks of her ass in 1992, when *Waiting to Exhale* came out. Terry McMillan wove a homespun tale about four black women—Robin, Bernadine, Gloria, and Savannah—and the consequences some of them suffered for the choices they made, especially their choices of men.

Did McMillan really put black men down? I don't think so. Her book actually delivered a backhanded slap at sisters' questionable judgment in affairs of the heart. But more than anything else, the fact that the book cast some black male characters in an unflattering light is what pissed off so many black men. Some people, such as Myles Johnson, a brother in Morristown, New Jersey, saw *Waiting to Exhale* as male bashing in buppie chic, "just another facet of the assassination of the black male character."

"Black writers do have a responsibility to be good storytellers," Johnson told me recently. "However, they do not operate in a vacuum. Every single thing that they write impacts on the group as a whole. I'm not disputing that Terry may have had bad experiences with some black men. But it's unfair to take those experiences and use them as an indictment against all black men. Terry's work may be therapeutic for her, but there must be a balance. If you're showing one side of black men, where is the flip side? Where is *my* portrayal? I don't behave like those men in her book."

What is ironic is that without being aware of it, many of the blacks who criticize the way African Americans are portrayed are doing the very thing we accuse whites of doing to us: using the twisted behaviors of a few people to make judgments about the entire race. We know that most black men are strong, noble brothers who struggle as hard as anybody else to make the most of a messed-up situation in America. If we truly know this, then it seems we should be able to accept isolated stories about disturbed or oppressive black men as just that—isolated tales that don't reflect our total reality.

Instead of being so defensive about negative portrayals of black men, maybe we ought to look around and ask ourselves, *Is this story true in part or in whole?* If much of what's written is even partly reflective of our reality, then critics should back off, cool out, chill.

"Unfortunately, the black people who are the most militant

are the ones who seem to be more hung up than anybody on what white people think," Terry McMillan said in an interview with *Publishers Weekly.* "[Critics say], 'We're airing our dirty laundry, why can't we portray ourselves more positively?' . . . They make the assumption that we're anthropologists, sociologists, psychologists, when all we are is storytellers. They try to put this weight on our shoulders, which I totally dismiss."

The disturbing thing is that in the cases of McMillan and Walker, the criticism they got may have affected them enough to influence their subsequent works. Even now—fifteen years after *The Color Purple* was published—Walker is still arguing that the book and the movie were misunderstood. She was so disturbed by what she considered the public's misinterpretation that she devoted most of her latest book, *The Same River Twice,* to the trauma she went through. In one chapter, Walker actually reprints the complete unused version of the screenplay of *The Color Purple.* It's as if she wants to prove to the public that the movie conveyed a different message than she intended to convey.

For her part, McMillan found a more subtle way to redeem herself. Her latest novel, *How Stella Got Her Groove Back,* is about a career woman who vacations in Jamaica and falls in love with a dude half her age. He turns out to be a more positive male character, somebody who comes across as the complete opposite of some of the no-count men in *Exhale*.

It's no put-down of McMillan and Walker that they were troubled by the accusation that they were somehow "traitors to the race" because of what they wrote. It's hard not to be affected by that kind of heat. And the criticism must have been especially hard to take because it was so undeserved. Still, McMillan, in the interview with *Publishers Weekly*, seemed determined to stand her ground: "I said exactly what I meant, and I'm not apologizing for any of it."

Alice Walker responded in a milder tone, even though the criticism heaped on McMillan was lightweight compared with that she received. In *The Same River Twice*, she wrote:

The attacks, many of them personal and painful, continued for many years, right alongside the praise, the prizes, the Oscar award nominations. I often felt isolated, deliberately misunderstood and alone. . . . I accepted it with all the grace and humor I possessed. Still, there is no denying the pain of being not simply challenged publicly, but condemned. It was said that I hated men, black men in particular; that my work was injurious to black male and female relationships; that my ideas of equality and tolerance were harmful, even destructive to the black community. . . . I eventually sought temporary refuge in Mexico, where I was able to work in peace. By then I had grown used to seeing my expressions taken out of context, rearranged, distorted. It was a curious experience that always left me feeling as if I had ingested poison.

The irony in all the criticism, I feel, is that so many black community "activists" came out, unified and powerful, to protest the negative black male images in *The Color Purple,* yet nobody can seem to find those activists when their help is needed on other, more crucial fronts. For years now, gangsta rappers have bombarded our senses with profane, sexist songs and videos that celebrate the very worst in black behavior—male and female. But there's barely a public whimper from the so-called activists who clamored so loudly for Alice Walker's head. It smells like hypocrisy and cowardice to me.

When it comes to assessing how African Americans are portrayed in literature and in popular culture in general, it sometimes seems that black folks aren't sure exactly *what* we want. We say we want to see more positive images of blacks, but even when we get those images, we tend to find fault in those portrayals as well.

Take, for instance, *The Cosby Show.* In all the years it was on the air, I couldn't count the number of times I heard blacks complain that Bill Cosby's sitcom about a black doctor, a black lawyer, and their family was bogus. Here was a show that gave us a positive alternative to the bug-eyed, chicken-and-biscuit-eating black folks we saw on TV in previous decades, and some people still weren't pleased.

The main complaint among its critics was *The Cosbys are unreal. Black people don't live like that.* The reality is some black people do live "like that." What's more, *The Cosby Show,* and other black shows, for that matter, should not be saddled with the responsibility of having to depict how *all* black people live. Black people are not monolithic—not any more than white people are.

I got a mild taste of that kind of erratic criticism in 1994 when I published my memoir, *Makes Me Wanna Holler.* Before it came out, I'd often heard folks complain that mainstream presses refused to publish works by black men. A good number of black female writers, including Walker, McMillan, Toni Morrison, and Maya Angelou, were being published regularly by such presses. But it was said that despite the success of writers like James Baldwin, John Edgar Wideman, John A. Williams, and others, black men were hard-pressed to get their stories in print. Among blacks, the general suspicion was that mainstream publishers didn't want to give voice to the militancy and racial hostility that black male writers often express.

But after my book came out, the conspiracy theories

shifted into a different gear. Steeped in the colored logic, some black folks complained that *Makes Me Wanna Holler* was proof that publishers would print stories by black men only if they contained "pathology," gory details about sex, crime, and general mayhem. That same complaint had been leveled when filmmaker John Singleton wrote and directed the now urban-classic *Boyz N the Hood.*

Damn. You can't please some people no matter *what* you do.

I view the pathology complaint as yet another indication of some black people's unwillingness to face our denial on many fronts. One reason black pathology is so persistent in our communities today is that we haven't confronted it squarely. Despite the evidence of widespread crime and violence we see in our communities every day, many blacks prefer to pretend that it doesn't exist, or they suggest that it's not as bad as whites say it is.

More than anything else, some black people's refusal to accept the reality of incest—even in a work of fiction such as *The Color Purple*—reveals that we're running away from some of our deepest problems. A psychologist friend said our denial stems from "a need to see white people as evil and perverted and black people as innocent and good. So sexual deviancy is a myth that we ascribe to white people. . . . From my perspective as a psychologist, I see cases of black incest every day, so I was wondering what the critics were talking about."

My biggest problem with gripes about Terry McMillan's and Alice Walker's writing is that critics seem to overlook the enormous good that those books have done. For sisters, those books provided a kind of therapy that's been hard to come by anywhere else. *The Color Purple* and *Waiting to Exhale* put black women's innermost struggles on center stage. They represent validation of black women's pain and struggles. They inspired a whole lot of soul-searching by black women, who wrestle with an array of complex social issues in trying to define their relationships—as mothers, sisters, aunts, daughters, and lovers—with black men. As Michele Wallace pointed out in *Black Macho,* much of the previous literature about black women reflected the broader public view of them as superwomen. They've been portrayed as fat Sapphires who were put on this earth to shoulder the many burdens of their families and their men. In this warped vision, black women either don't have personal needs or they happily submerge their needs and ambitions for the sake of the greater black good.

As the colored logic goes, Alice Walker would've been much better off writing about mean old white people committing incest. It's possible, though, that *because* she wrote about incest among blacks, some African-American victims might be more inclined to get the help they need in order to heal. Likewise, with *Waiting to Exhale,* scores of black women wrestling with tough issues of career, family, and men could celebrate their struggles and take comfort in knowing that they're not alone.

Finally, without being preachy, these books provided informal road maps to help black women overcome their massive challenges. In *The Color Purple,* Celie triumphed over her fear of her oppressor. In *Waiting to Exhale,* each of the four female characters took control of her life, whether the men cooperated in that process or not. In both cases, the authors essentially told women that men have no more power over their lives and their happiness than the power women give them.

Picasso once said, "Art is a lie which makes us realize the truth." We need to accept stories about black life for what they are: On one level, they're art—entertaining and often fictitious stories; at the same time, they're blunt truths, literary accounts of the pain that we suffer—and inflict on one another—every day.

The bottom line is we *need* black writers to air our dirty laundry. We also need those writers to resist pressure to sugarcoat black reality. Lord knows we need that for all our sakes.

3

MEN: WE JUST DON'T GET IT

At about the tender age of sixteen, I carried around in my wallet a wrinkled piece of paper that contained a notorious list. I'm ashamed to admit it now, but back then I proudly showed off the contents of that list, often during wine-bingeing bragging sessions with the boys on the block.

The list contained the names of some twenty or so teenage girls—in our vernacular, babes, broads, bitches—who held the unlucky distinction of having been laid by me.

In most cases, I had "talked the drawers off" the girls, meaning they'd willingly yielded to empty promises designed to persuade them to prove their devotion by hopping into bed. But a few girls named on that list had been strong-armed—sexually assaulted—by me.

It never occurred to me during that time to distinguish between those girls on the list who'd willingly consented to sex and those who had not. The names of actual rape victims were jotted down on that smudgy piece of paper tucked between my driver's license and my Social Security card. There was enough written evidence of confessed sex crimes, scribbled in my distinctive handwriting, to put me away in prison for a long, long time.

But that didn't matter to me then. I wasn't afraid of exposure because I honestly didn't grasp the tragic implications of the thing. I just didn't get it.

That might seem unbelievable, but what's more stunning is this: I was far from alone in such cruel stupidity. Of course, there were many exceptions. There were lots of decent, self-respecting teenage boys who wouldn't dare take advantage of a girl even if the opportunity presented itself. Still, in addition to my hoodlum partners and me, a sizable number of other, "regular" dudes—bookworms, jocks, and other everyday, play-by-the-rules kinds of guys—also held cloudy notions about the distinction between consensual sex and rape.

I've heard all the macho men's-room talk, and I'd say the number of boys and men who harbor blurry notions about the liberties they can rightfully take with a female is nothing less than mind-boggling. If the truth be told, on some level of awareness or another, most men don't get it.

That massive male blindness accounts for the boatload of sexual-harassment cases filed by women in government and civilian workplaces every year. That obtuseness explains why some of the highest-ranking men in the nation—including the President of the United States and a U.S. Supreme Court justice—have been accused of taking indecent liberties with women.

William Kennedy Smith, Mike Tyson, the late Tupac Shakur—theirs are among the high-profile sexual-assault cases that have made headlines in recent years, but they represent only a small fraction of the incidents that do untold psychic damage to girls and women every day.

From this male's perspective, the pervasiveness of men's problem with sexual aggression suggests one of two things: Either God developed a defective sensibility gene when he assembled males, or there's a major flaw in our cultural conditioning, and that flaw feeds this madness that's corrupted us.

After much soul-searching, I'm inclined to believe the latter is true: that even in these so-called modern times, we still uphold a supermacho cultural climate that helps men feel comfortable—even justified—in forcing their attentions on the opposite sex. Certainly, the role of individual responsibility can't be dismissed, but in a sense our whole society is an accessory in this thing called rape. In America, where sex seems to sell everything, from new cars to good beer, it's not hard at all to become a sexist pig. All that's needed are eyes, ears, and a hearty store of testosterone.

As I look back on my own warped past, it's impossible to say just when the boorishness toward females first kicked in. I suspect that for me and for most other boys who mistakenly embraced sex as a rite of passage into manhood, the foundation for our brutish ways was laid early and deep.

Long before Tonka trucks and G.I. Joes assigned us our sex roles, we boys were sent clear messages about who we were to become. The sex-typed toys that we were cheerfully given at Christmastime simply reinforced the negative stereotypes that we were already being force-fed every day.

It's very likely that adolescence was the time when the crass sexism seeped in deeper for my buddies and me. Maybe it was somewhere around middle school—when zealous cheerleaders leaped in the air and did phenomenal splits in support of the boys' more celebrated exploits on the football field—that we were thoughtlessly handed the double standards that would govern us.

Somewhere amid all the TV ads showing half-naked buxom women selling products that had absolutely nothing to do with the female body, the notion of male dominance crystallized: While the girls learned to view males as the objects of their love, we boys learned to regard females as mere objects.

For many guys, that notion creates a major emotional disconnect. That disconnect makes it easier to regard females as something less on the human scale. Once that disconnect occurs, it's entirely possible to discount a female's humanity; it's entirely possible to subject a woman to sexual harassment or, worse, to rape.

For my buddies and me, our inclination to strong-arm girls related directly to our definition of masculinity. Men, who are schooled by other men, are taught to see themselves, first and foremost, as conquerors. Our movie heroes attest to that. Heros such as John Wayne were almost always big, strong, domineering men who often boasted a sharp, sexist wit. In their movies, the settings, story lines, and subplots were secondary to the underlying quest. The bottom line was obvious. It was about pussy: The conqueror got the pretty girl.

That's how the fellas and I thought of it, too. We didn't think of what we did as rape as much as we saw it as the ultimate macho conquest sport. Our competitive language reinforced that. In the male idiom, where men were called "hounds" and women were dubbed "foxes," it required no great leap of logic to extend the realm of conquest to sex. Life's purpose was made clear: The hunt was on, and females were the game.

As teenagers, operating with that kind of twisted vision as a frame of reference, we singled out as potential prey every little cute thing who even *thought* she had a crush on one of us. (Strangely enough, females in our families—mothers, sisters, cousins, and so on—were afforded respect.) With few exceptions, everybody's "phat" daughter who crossed our path was an unwitting candidate for our respective lists.

And why not keep a list? Almost from day one, we boys had been primed to score.

What is clearer now than it was back then is that the social scientists' take on rape is absolutely true: It's more about power than about sexual enjoyment. Think about it; nobody in his right mind can truly enjoy forcing someone to share something so intimate as sex.

Sometimes, the fellas and I engaged in the conquest sport alone, but we occasionally formed teams that carried out a male rite called "running trains." Often with the help of guys secretly stationed in closets in the appointed room, we simply intimidated our victims with fear or might or both, then took turns having our way.

It was a perverse exercise in male bonding; it was a bizarre camaraderie that boys and men shared as a way of showing off; it was a reenactment of the primitive caveman's rite of dividing the spoils of the hunt.

Really, we didn't get it.

Probably the clearest indication of our utter confusion about the seriousness of sexual aggression was the conflicting attitudes we held about rape. If you'd walked into the very room at the very moment one of our sexual escapades was going down, we would've been highly offended—pissed off even—at any suggestion that we were committing a serious crime.

It's true. We frowned on rapists. We regarded rapists as deranged men, social misfits, outcasts, freaks who were so hard up they couldn't get sex on their own. Reports by the American Medical Association show that 80 percent of rape victims know their assailants. But in our limited vision, rapists were people who attacked perfect strangers to get their jollies off. Rapists were weirdos who went alone to darkened theaters, slouched low in their seats, and masturbated while gazing at the movie screen.

Looking back, I find it hard to know exactly where the moral breakdown occurred. I suspect that it erupted somewhere amid all those puzzling instructions that were handed down to us boys from men who were no more than grown-up boys themselves. Where females were concerned, we boys were given general training about right and wrong, but we also were granted broad latitude to interpret what a woman's rights *really* are.

I now know this: A woman has the right to say no whenever she wants. A woman has the right to change her mind anytime she chooses. But I remember being told, straight up, from men I respected, that it's OK for a man to take sexual liberties with a woman if she "leads him on." I recall hearing, over and over, that a woman is required to "give it up" if a man spends a fair amount of money on her during a date.

Indications are that the notions my buddies and I were taught back then are still being passed along today. In an AMA survey of high school students, 56 percent of the girls and 76 percent of the boys believed forced sex was acceptable "under some circumstances." Among eleven- to fourteen-year-olds, 51 percent of the boys and 41 percent of the girls said forced sex was acceptable if the boy "spent a lot of money" on the girl.

And so much of what we were told was male ego driven. We were assured that, regardless of what they say to the contrary, most girls and women really *want* to have sex: "They just need to be coaxed along."

If all this strikes you as appalling, then try this next thought on for size: Where the general oppression of females is concerned, there are also a good number of women unwittingly playing supporting roles. There is some subtle and blatant voodoo being worked on them that even a whole lot of young girls and grown-up women *just don't get*.

That includes the vast number of women who squeal in excited glee at men flaunting the same macho behaviors that victimize them; that includes the Miss America wanna-bes who strut across lighted stages in high heels and swimsuits so men can judge their considerable "talents"; that certainly includes the pseudodivas who shake their rounded rumps for those gold-chained misogynists in some rap-music videos.

It's no mystery why so many females are so gullible. While the boys were conditioned to be sexist oafs, the girls were socialized to seek happiness by providing the services men value most. Almost from birth, they are well primed by the likes of Barbie dolls and Suzy Homemakers to cooperate in this sex-oppression thing.

"Our parents gave us girls tea sets for Christmas," Debra Dennis, a friend, told me recently. "And we didn't even drink tea in our *fucking* house!"

The females were hit with it nonstop. Still are. And you *have* to know that for young girls there's a cumulative effect of seeing so many women everywhere serving so many men's interests—all the time. At some point, the message sinks in: Gals exist for the sole purpose of pleasing guys.

All that bull, piled high as the heavens, made it easier for my buddies and me to get our way. And the confusion that those messages created in young girls' heads is what enabled us to get away undetected with the things we did.

It's no wonder, then, that the AMA survey found that

among college-age women who have been the victim of rape or attempted rape, 42 percent never even reported what happened to them.

Like so many others, my partners and I usually got away scot-free, usually without being punished for sexual assaults. But in the years since then, I've often wondered whether any of us *really* got away.

Life has a way of avenging folks who've been terribly wronged, even if the victims never get a chance to witness poetic justice firsthand. Life has a way of revisiting you with acts of meanness that you may have committed against someone in some long-forgotten time. Among the guys in my bunch, some got their wickedness shipped right back to them, almost exactly the same way they'd dished it out.

When I consider this idea, I'm reminded of something that happened during one of our street-corner bragging sessions years ago. A number of dudes were standing around in a tight circle, listening to a guy called Foots gloat over some girl he'd strong-armed the night before. A dude I'll call Alfred Towns, who'd also been known to do such things, happened to walk up and join the circle. Foots was so wrapped up in his boasting that he didn't even see Alfred approach. He went on jabbering.

And Alfred went on listening—only to get what must've

been the shock of his life: Alfred heard Foots call out his sister's name.

When Foots spotted Alfred in the crowd, he smiled sheepishly and apologized. As everyone turned and looked his way, Alfred stared straight ahead. His eyes glazed over, and he stood in stunned silence. Alfred was deeply affected; he was shocked to learn that his own sister had been raped.

In the years since those crazy days, I've changed my thinking about women and sex, but still, life's revenge has come back to haunt me, too. The first time revenge paid a visit, I was involved with a woman I *really* felt strongly about. In one of our intimate conversations, she disclosed that some guys had run a train on her years ago, when she was a teen. Another time, a former girlfriend confessed that she had once been "taken advantage of" by her boyfriend in a violent episode that left her permanently scarred.

These stories hurt me. But more than anything, they forced me to face my own past cruelty and helped me understand the truth about what I'd done: I had committed one of the worst offenses one person can commit against another and somehow had failed to see the brutality inherent in it. I just didn't get it.

Those stories told by my women friends also underscored just how widespread assaults on females are. They revealed that sexual violence is no respecter of color, race, or social standing, that it happens in all quarters, from church pews, where preachers take liberties with female members of their unsuspecting flocks, to college campuses, where frat brothers often carry on such manhood rites at the expense of hapless coeds.

Of all the life experiences that have taught me about the common threat to females' humanity, none has provided greater enlightenment than fatherhood. I think the Creator devised the best way to help me fully get the point when he gave me a daughter. She's twelve now and fast approaching that stage when boys and men will start eyeing her with that certain hungry look.

I look at her with a father's love—and also with a father's dread. As a man, I know what young predators might see when they look at her. They might see a vivacious, trusting little girl who is a stranger to no one. Or they might see a babe, a broad, a bitch, an object whose good nature makes her easy prey—a candidate for somebody's sordid list.

And I fear that my daughter may just fall for some boy who she thinks cares the world for her. He could be a nice guy. Or he could turn out to be another messed-up young man who, like me, was improperly schooled in matters of respect and sex. He might be another male who *just doesn't get it*.

4

GANGSTAS, GUNS, AND SHOOT-'EM-UPS

I'll never forget the first time I went with some of my partners to check out the movie version of Mario Puzo's classic, *The Godfather*. No telling how many violent films we'd seen before that one, but for us *The Godfather* was the serious *joint*.

Gangsters, guns, and violence have always fascinated Americans, and young blacks like us clearly were no different. We were mesmerized by *The Godfather*, mainly because its machine-gun shoot-outs and retaliatory murders among competing families took the thrill of gang warfare to an entirely new level.

We were most impressed by the code of principles that governed movie gangsters' lives. These characters had a way of resolving conflict that was appealing to us as teenage boys trying to work through the murky rites of manhood. The message that we picked up from the flick was, if somebody double-crosses you, he must be punished; and if somebody disrespects you, he deserves to die.

I remember staring at the movie screen and thinking, *Yeah, that's right. He deserves to die!* When the movie ended, my partners and I agreed that it was the hippest flick we'd ever seen. Afterward, we stepped outdoors, inspired and hyped. We were so hyped that we bopped boldly down the sidewalk, talking loud and intentionally bumping into people—hoping somebody would protest and give us an excuse to enact a bare-knuckled version of the violence we'd just seen on the movie screen.

We were young and impressionable, barely able to separate movie fantasy from fact. *The Godfather* was fantasy. But to a bunch of spirited boys trying to define themselves and identify with a group, it was a grand celebration of machismo.

By then, we'd already begun hanging on the block. We rumbled in the streets, and when we got older, we turned to guns to settle scores. Throughout it all, the principles we picked up in *The Godfather* stayed with us. They blended nicely with other macho, street-corner values filtering into our heads.

I eventually got my chance to do the *Godfather* thing when an older thug in the neighborhood threatened my girl. To my way of thinking, that dude had offended my lady, and by extension, he'd disrespected me. I concluded, *He deserves to die.*

I was nineteen, and it didn't take much more than a notion at that age to push me into reckless action. When I ran into that dude again, I pulled out my pistol and gunned him down.

From the moment I pulled the trigger, it was like one great fantasy. It was as glorious as the gangland slayings in the movie I'd seen. After the dude collapsed, I stood over him, proud that I'd properly handed out street justice. I'd upheld the code of *Godfather* principles I'd embraced.

Later that night, I wound up in a police station, being fingerprinted and booked. That's when fantasy faded and reality kicked in. That's when the real me resurfaced. Suddenly, I was forced to shed my pseudogangster image and come to grips with who I really was: a silly, scared teenager who was mixed up in the head.

Lucky for me, the dude survived. I went to court and was sentenced to thirty days in jail and a three-hundred-dollar fine—a light sentence that amounted to a grand stroke of luck. But in the years since then, I have never stopped thinking about that shooting and the influences that led me to do such things.

I thought about those influences recently, after the gangland murders of Biggie Smalls and Tupac Shakur, two hugely popular rap artists whose musical fantasies were played out in the streets. For me, those influences also come to mind when I read about public debates over the fantasy violence reflected in some rap music and the real violence ravaging black communities everywhere. I have to admit that the sad reality of our times forces me to agree with folks who say that, literally, this fantasy thing is killing us.

"There's a real thin line between fantasy and reality," Chuck D, a rapper with the group Public Enemy told me recently. "As black people, we ain't in control of our reality. When you're not in control of your reality, fantasy becomes a bigger influence."

Chuck is one of a number of concerned hip-hop artists who agree that "issues in [negative] rap need to be addressed." He and other socially conscious rappers are among a handful of people trying to rescue rap from its downwardly spiraling public image as the music of dark messengers delivering grim bulletins of hopelessness and doom. Those bulletins became a lot more real when Tupac and Biggie were gunned down.

Of course, not all rap is bad. In fact, I like it a lot; much of it is so creative that it makes me shout. I absolutely fell in love with rap when it first came out. Here was a brilliant style of music created right in the streets of the urban hood by the very people society dismisses as worthless and dumb.

The early rap seemed hip because a lot of it was simply funny. We black folks have often relied on humor to get us through tough times. The emergence of early rappers such as the Sugar Hill Gang and Grandmaster Flash was a throwback to the days when brothers on street corners recited the comical exploits of fictitious characters such as the Signifying Monkey, Shine, and Dolomite.

I also dug rap because, among young blacks, it showed the promise to become a tremendous social force. (After all, rap is political, and politics is rap.) Like the protest music of the '60s, rap burst onto the scene partly in response to an oppressively conservative culture, in this case the renewed, more blatant oppression of the Reagan era. Using snappy rhymes mixed with staccato beats, such groups as Public Enemy blasted the white-controlled system; with unflinching candor, they often analyzed the veiled, complex maneuverings of Washington politicians and broke them down for common folks' comprehension. They pinpointed precisely the powerful correlation between racist laws passed on Capitol Hill and their crushing impact in urban hoods.

When it first hit the streets, rap had the potential to inspire a new generation of young bloods to strive to be even more militant and even more independent of the white power structure than the black radicals who preceded them. In short, rap made it hip for young folks to be politically conscious again.

The broad appeal of rap also emerged as a scorching indictment of mainstream black leadership. In these times, when so many black leaders have been silenced or enticed to go along to get along, young people have grown impatient. They see too few black leaders taking bold public stands, fighting aggressively to counteract conservatives' systematic assaults.

By contrast, rappers come *raw*. They give many disenchanted young blacks the image of a leader they crave: somebody who'll stand up to the white man, speak his mind and make it plain. "Whether it's right or wrong, rappers are saying shit," Chuck D pointed out during a detailed discussion. "We dialogue about what's going on, but nobody else is speaking out."

Make no mistake about it. Rap represents the voice of the powerless, the forgotten, the dispossessed. Among many blacks, rappers are viewed as lyrical Malcolm Xs, fiery orators come to liberate oppressed African Americans who say they're fed up—fed up with discrimination, fed up with Uncle Toms and Clarence Thomases, fed up with being systematically fucked with, fucked around, and fucked over.

You have to admire them for being on the case, challenging the status quo the way they do. But there's one major problem here: With the passage of time, something ugly has seeped into some forms of rap. Some of the folks who represent this slick style of music have transformed it into something ruthless—so much so that rappers who once sang about being oppressed now sound insanely oppressive themselves and downright cruel.

Check out this old rap by Just Ice:

> Faggots, bitches,
> Look how their ass switches,
> They see Just(ice) come
> and they move before they get stitches
> Persistent, insistent
> nothing changed, nothing different
> A bullet or a bat,
> Just pick it.

As a friend observed recently, "Some rap is clever and crafty, but when you really analyze it, it's the most public display of internalized oppression and pathology that I've ever seen."

The reason for the grotesque transformation is quite simple: Rap has become a victim of its own success. In the '80s, groups such as 2 Live Crew gained a lot of wealth and notoriety by being vulgar and vile. Ever since then, other rappers have joined in; they simply copied 2 Live Crew's formula and turned up the profanity a notch or two. In the competition to stand out from the broadening bunch of overnight sensations who gained fame by merely talking shit, rappers struggled to create more vulgar rhymes that had more shock value—and more commercial appeal—than those of their competitors. In the process, some also relied more heavily on fantasy violence to get a hit; it became their creative crutch, a showy gimmick designed to attract young listeners, who are titillated by braggadocio and dirty words.

The result is that the messages of those rappers who may actually have something positive and meaningful to say are too often drowned out by gangsta rap. In gangsta rap, which was popularized by the group N.W.A. (Niggaz With Attitude) in the late 1980s, anarchy and murder rule the day. Consider this catchy piece of advice from an old hit by former N.W.A. member Dr. Dre, and imagine how it might sound to a young boy's ears:

> Rat-a-tat and a tat like that
> Never hesitate to put a nigga on his back.

Plain and simple, that's a boastful call for black men to kill one another, *Godfather* style. Among young blacks, lyrics such as these are so common that they've become the accepted norm. To me, they clearly demonstrate that gangsta rap is one aspect of hip-hop that ain't so hip.

At a time when young black men are killing one another with much more proficiency than the Ku Klux Klan, the immense popularity of gangsta rap makes you wonder whether the young blacks of this generation have lost their minds: *Why,* you ask, *would they embrace musical messages that celebrate the destruction of their own people? And why would they try to emulate the behavior of the very worst elements in black communities?*

There are a couple of reasons. First, as mentioned earlier, black people share the rest of America's fascination with the Mafia. The names of some of the most popular rappers attest to that: Mobb Deep, Scarface, Goodfellas, Capone -n- Noreaga, Wise Guyz, Godfather Don, Junior M.A.F.I.A. Even the record labels that produce rap reflect the kind of obsession with gangster toughness played out in the *Godfather* classic I saw years ago: Death Row Records, Bad Boy Entertainment, Ruthless Records, Threat Records, Penalty Records, Surrender Records.

In America, music always reflects the times. The steady emergence of gangsta rap is a clear sign that we're knee-deep in a mean-spirited, selfish age—in the past, we loved Lassie, the gentle collie that would save your life, first in the movies, then on prime-time TV. In today's America, Lassie is passé.

The pit bull is now the dog of choice. Likewise, whereas the black crooners of the past—the Temptations, the Supremes, and Gladys Knight—bespoke a period of general civility and love, gangsta rap symbolizes the coarse rudeness and proud hatred that's standard today.

Gangsta rap is also immensely popular because it's politically extremist, subversive, more cathartic than other rap. It feeds young blacks' yearning for open rebellion against a white mainstream that promotes inequality and a black mainstream that tolerates it.

Gangsterism, then, is presented as a radical political response to racism, and gangsta rappers are seen as de facto politicians for black America—*New Jack* leaders, revolutionaries who are bolder and more relevant than their predecessors.

And here is where the confusion *really* kicks in for many young folks: From gangsta rap, they do get an accurate analysis of black people's social problems, but that analysis is often followed by faulty solutions. In the past, values and solutions were often transmitted from elders to the young. With rap, values are imparted mainly from young people to their peers. As a result, young people often take in immature advice. Drug dealing, for instance, is offered as the answer to poverty, unemployment, the conservative agenda, and any other forces perceived as oppressive to blacks. Gangsterism is sold as a better, more defiant alternative to slaving for a white system that barely hides its contempt for black lives and black aspirations.

And of course, white folks constantly give rappers lots of ammo to support their case. The get-tough anti-crime and prison movement—which produced the wholesale jailing of so many young black men—provides beaucoup white villains for rappers to point fingers at. The conservative leaders on Capitol Hill, who spearheaded that movement, stand as convincing proof that white conspiracies do, in fact, continue to exist. Using the whole pathetic group of local, state, and national politicians who won election in recent years by opposing affirmative action and portraying black women as welfare queens, some rappers make a persuasive case to young black fans that, given the permanence of racism, street hustling is justified. *Don't even bother tryin' to make it in the white man's system. It's stacked! The gangsta life is the way to go. Deal drugs, carjack, kill, live large, die young, and along the way give the white man the finger.*

Rappers make it clear that for the new generation the old-school methods of racial progress are outdated. The notion that blacks can best get ahead by moving into, and up in, the mainstream is no longer appealing. Like the rappers Diamond and the Psychotic Neurotics, young blacks today will tell you in a heartbeat that they'd rather be self-employed than work for the white man:

> I told my boss about my plans
> And said I wanna be my own man
> A-yo, I know you put me on
> But yo, I gotta quit
> I want my own shit.

It's clear that they have the right idea: Black folks *do* need to be more independent. But again, the solution for economic independence is often way off track. For instance, in the album released after his death, Biggie Smalls, who sold crack in New York before he became a rapper, actually included a song that offers tips on how to be successful in the drug game. Titled "Ten Crack Commandments," the song gives this advice to young, potential businessmen: Don't give credit, don't carry large quantities of the stuff on you, don't use your own drugs, and

> This rule is so underrated
> Keep your family and business completely separated.

In the absence of bold voices of reason to openly challenge such crazy thinking, a good number of young blacks actually take their cues from gangsta rap. And why not? Young people assume, naturally, that if the rappers' social analysis is correct, then their proposed solutions must also be on the mark. "But the solutions are not knowledge based and experience based," Kim Dailey, a friend of mine, observed. "Most gangsta rappers are *young*. What do they know about solutions?"

That's what concerns Chuck D and other rappers who want to see the art used to enhance, rather than undermine, black survival. At the age of thirty-seven, Chuck is considered one of the elder statesmen of rap. He thinks his age and experience also qualify him to know the difference between music that heals and music that kills. "I'm an advocate for hip-hop as an art form," he told me. "It's not a bad thing for art to have a borderline. We want people to say what they feel, but we also want people to speak with the right information. A lot of what some rappers say really doesn't deserve any exposure."

Anybody who understands the nature of rap knows that it's more than mere witty rhymes. It's a phenomenon. It's the central part of an unorganized but powerful cultural movement called hip-hop that influences the way young blacks walk, talk, dress, and think.

To comprehend the sheer force of rap, you've got to listen to it closely and experience its lure. It's characterized by a driving, pulsating beat, accompanied by lyrical slang that's angrily barked, not sung.

The key element is aggression—in rappers' body language, tone, and clever lyrics. It often leaves listeners hyped, on edge, pissed off—about *something*. Maybe that was the case with Ray Howard, who at nineteen was sentenced to death in Austin, Texas, for fatally shooting a state trooper. Howard said that on the night he killed the trooper, he was hyped from listening to the hard-core rhythms of Tupac Shakur, the Geto Boys, and Ganksta N-I-P.

Of course, the most important element in gangsta rap is its themes, which are hammered through different songs with awesome beats. Those themes center largely on these ideas: Women are no more than bitches and hos, disposable playthings that exist merely for men's abusive delight; it's cool to use violence and any other means necessary to get what you want; and, just like the message I picked up from *The God-father—if somebody disses you, he deserves to die.*

Over and over, gangsta rappers toast toughness and promote the notion that the kind of cold-bloodedness reflected in many senseless street murders today is an expression of manhood; they say it's admirable to be hard, unfeeling toward the world. Underlying all the tough talk is a deep depression, an angry, suicidal pessimism about life and an eerie preoccupation with death and dying. Check out this boast by rapper Just Ice:

> Don't try to get too close
> and try to kiss me and hug me
> start to caress me, then say you love me.
> 'Cause I don't feel shit
> It's only rhythm that I ride
> The only love I got is psychopathic homicide.

The potency in gangsta rap comes partly from the repetition of those kinds of messages. The same negative themes and the identical gangsta images are repeated so often among rappers in videos that one comedian said he thought there was only one video created to represent all rap tunes.

The typical gangsta-rap video resembles one put out by the late Biggie Smalls. In that video, we see Biggie lying in bed conducting business on a cellular phone while two naked women, his hos, fawn on him. The message in this and similar videos is clear: You can lie in bed, operate your illicit business enterprises, and make millions—all by being a player, a slick gangster.

It's the American dream gone amok with the misguided notion of what the writer Amiri Baraka calls "primitive capitalism." It's the *Godfather* fantasy, '90s style. It's subliminal seduction at its very worst.

Dr. William Byrd, a black clinical psychologist, pointed out that for young, impressionable people the mere fact that explicit gangsta lyrics are aired on the radio lends credence to their message as truth. "When you bombard someone with those messages, it causes conflict, even within those young people who may have been taught other values. With these rap messages, not only are they being bombarded with radio, they also get video. So it's what you hear *and* what you see. It confirms that these are acceptable values in a subculture. Children reason that if the society as a whole doesn't accept it, then they wouldn't put it on the air."

Nobody can deny the awesome power the electronic media wield. With sixty-second TV spots, advertisers persuade people to go out and buy products they don't even need; with messages repeated over radio airwaves, politicians affect people's views and voting picks. These advertisers, politicians, and others pay billions of dollars a year to get their messages out over the air. They'd love to have the round-the-clock exposure that rap music gets.

Among many older blacks, there's an acute feeling of déjà vu in all this gangster worship. There's a frightening sense that we haven't learned from history. In the 1970s, Hollywood gave us such blaxploitation classics as *Shaft, Superfly,* and *The Mack,* all glamorizing life on the streets. The stars of those movies became cultural icons who set the tone for many young blacks' fashions and values (mine included) and even influenced the kinds of cars they bought. (The car of choice was a luxury ride with "gangster" whitewalls.)

Many African Americans hailed those flicks as new opportunities for blacks in film. But now, when we look back at that period, we tend to take a different view. When we see photos of ourselves as cocky young clowns in wide-brimmed hats and platform shoes, it's clear that in the '70s, Hollywood gave us little more than a foolish fantasy—the movies gave us a chance to make jesters of ourselves. When the novelty of black gangsters faded and box-office receipts fell, movie houses dropped black actors like a bad habit, and many blacks later realized we'd unwittingly cooperated in our own exploitation.

Chuck D believes, as I do, that the white-run record industry is doing today what the white-run movie industry did back in the '70s—it's profiting from young blacks' self-hatred and ignorance. "The low road is easier to walk upon as a recording artist. A lot of rappers wouldn't get the time of day from record producers if they weren't doing negative rap. . . . There's a system that benefits from this. . . . White corporations out there make a lot of money from rap; then they go off to their well-established communities, and black people are the casualties at the end of the day."

Young bloods nowadays tend to snicker when they see

shots of *Superfly* guys from back in the day. They also fail to recognize the parallels: In the current videos, many of the brash young players sporting gangster brims and gold rope chains look like new age buffoons. And some of the portraits rappers project are as racist and destructive as anything the '70s blaxploitation films produced.

From conversations with young people, including rappers themselves, I think I've heard all the justifications of gangsta rap and the blunt denials of the harm it does. I have yet to hear a sound defense of this form of music.

Many rappers say it's crazy to tie music to behavior. But the history of African Americans shows that that's not quite true. From slavery times on up to the present, music has always played a big role in what black folks think and do. Slaves often sang spirituals to help them endure the pain of bondage. They used those same songs to relate plans to rebel or escape. And in the 1960s and '70s, old-school musicians such as James Brown urged us over the airwaves to "Say It Loud: 'I'm Black and I'm Proud,' " and they helped transform black people's self-loathing into racial pride.

It's true that, as rap's defenders say, other complex social factors are mainly to blame for black-on-black violence: public apathy, parental neglect, the allure of drugs and guns, to name a few. But those are accessories. They don't address the *mind-set* behind the madness. And more than anything else—

including the influence of mamas, daddies, preachers, and teachers—the mind-set of young blacks is tuned in to rap.

It's also true that for a lot of brothers and sisters in the urban hood, rap music validates the bleak realities they see and live every day. But by glamorizing those harsh realities, they promote black cruelty and suffering as the desired norm.

And yes, I know young suburban whites are among rap's biggest fans. But for white kids, hip-hop is just a cultural adventure. It's a brief outing. It's slumming—a risk-free safari into the urban jungle. Unlike blacks, who remain trapped in the hell depicted by rap, white kids can tune in to rap fantasies at will and return to the comforting reality of their privileged world anytime they want.

Of course, many young folks argue that the persuasive powers of gangsta rap are exaggerated by the media. As one defiant rapper said in a recent MTV interview, "The music doesn't cause the violence. Rap is only words."

That naïve response left me screaming—loudly—at the TV set. *Only words? Only words? Words, my man, run the world! Words start wars, and words create peace! Most violent skirmishes in the world start with words! Words set the tone for* actions, *fool!*

In the case of gangsta rap, some of the violent conflicts among rappers is proof of that. Those conflicts started several years ago, when rap first veered from its original course. At

the time, some MCs (microphone controllers) began recording boasts of their skills on the mike, hyping themselves at the
expense of competitors, whom they scorned as "sucker
MCs." The public ragging started with veiled references to
other rappers; then, the recorded put-downs became more
specific and more personal, with rappers bragging about how
they'd "beat down" competitors. Finally, some of those rappers ran into others at concerts. Manhood was defended.
Fights broke out. And it all started with *words*.

The now infamous bicoastal beef widely believed to be re-
sponsible for the deaths of Biggie Smalls and Tupac Shakur
was also sparked by words. It began with verbal sparring,
carried on through songs and videos with rappers from the
West Coast, primarily L.A., and rappers from the East Coast,
mainly New York, exchanging tough talk about who was the
more authentic gangsta, who was "fake," and who was really
a hard-core product of the hood. Somehow, Biggie, who represented the East Coast, and Tupac, a West Coast rap giant,
got entangled in their own war of words. That war got real
ugly when Tupac, using a Biggie Smalls look-alike, did a
video boasting of having had sex with Biggie's wife: *"I fucked
your bitch, you fat motherfucka!"*

It was the ultimate macho put-down. Sometime later,
Tupac was gunned down while sitting in a car at a stoplight
in Las Vegas. Almost six months to the day after Tupac's

death, Biggie Smalls, aka Notorious B.I.G., was killed gang-land style in Los Angeles—also while sitting in a car at a stop-light. The result is that two more multitalented black men are gone. Smoked. Wiped out. And it all started as trash-talking on vinyl; it all started with *words.*

"This East Coast–West Coast thing started out as fantasy," Chuck D said. "It's now a reality. Now, we can't get around the fact that people have actually died. That makes it harder to defend."

The proof of the influence of fantasy violence doesn't begin or end with the deaths of Tupac and Notorious B.I.G. There are many other, stronger correlations between negative rap and the gangster madness going on among young black men.

Black-on-black violence has always been a problem, but it has escalated sharply only since the 1980s, when gangsta rap became the major strain. Likewise, the sudden and sharp in-crease in the number of black juveniles gunning people down also corresponds with the rise of gangsta rap. This is impor-tant when you consider that juveniles are most impression-able, and they're the group least able to separate fantasy from fact.

And even if you argue that black-on-black drug wars ac-count for many of the murders, you still haven't explained the rapid rise in random violence unrelated to drugs. It happens in cities all the time. Like the young guy who, while cruising around with his buddies, declared that he felt "like smokin' somebody," then randomly killed a woman passing in a car.

It's no wonder that the madness is spreading. By its sheer pervasiveness, the gangsta-rap culture imposes a tremendous amount of peer pressure, even on young blacks who try to play it straight. In their songs and in their gangster personae, some rappers promote the notion that you're lame if you go to school; you're weak if you weren't raised slinging dope; you're nobody if you didn't come up hard. That message is reinforced so often and so powerfully that young blacks whose experiences don't reflect a life in the streets are made to feel they're somehow illegit.

That pressure is apparent in middle-class black suburban areas, where kids from so-called stable homes are ragged in rap songs because they lack street exploits to boast about. In the past, people were ashamed to say they came from the public-housing projects. Now, suburban kids go all out to create the false impression that they came up in the hood.

Even many black college students, who traditionally have stood apart from the street culture, have begun to give in to pressure to conform to the thug life. Visit some of the nation's premier black colleges, from Hampton University to the At-lanta University complex, and you'll see that it's hard to tell the difference between college kids and thugs on the block.

Many of them buy into the culture of obnoxiousness that is so pervasive among young blacks now.

In dress and manner, many students strive mightily to shake off rappers' musical portrayal of them as wimpy nerds. The males try to give the impression that they're really gangsta killas hiding out in college to duck the Man, and black college coeds commonly use exaggerated street slang, as if they were airheaded yo girls from around the way.

Some black students are so confused about where they stand that they even imitate the violence glamorized by gangsta rap. As a result, drug wars and turf battles at black colleges in recent years have led to more brawls, rapes, and campus shooting deaths than ever before. The silliness of the college turf wars can be seen on a black campus where I recently delivered a lecture. I learned that just days before I got there, a crew of students from New York had gotten into a brawl with a Detroit crew—and this was at a rural college in Kentucky!

To make things even worse, some female rappers have developed their own warped versions of the gangsta thing. In one song, a female rapper boasts of punching somebody "dead in the face." In another, a rapper says she's most attracted to "roughnecks."

And just as hard-core gangsta rap inspires the behavior of

many young black boys and men, some female listeners seem to be inspired, too. I'll never forget that a woman arrested a few years ago in connection with one of Florida's most brutal tourist slayings went by the nickname Gangsta Bitch.

Of course, the people who make the most convincing case for the negative influence of gangsta rap are some of the rappers themselves. It's clear that many of them believe their own hype. Some don't hesitate to act out their raps: Flavor Flav, Snoop Doggy Dogg, Slick Rick—the biggest and the best have been charged in sex- and violence-related incidents so many times that their arrests no longer come as a surprise.

I can't condemn them for getting into trouble with the law—I've been there myself. But these dudes use their criminal records as credentials to prove they're qualified to rap about the streets.

What's more, the lives of gangsta rappers are riddled with contradictions that they can't even *begin* to justify. There's Ice Cube, who one day embraces the virtues of self-reliance and clean living advocated by Louis Farrakhan and the next day is rapping about the power of Glocks, making fast money, and clockin' hos. There was Tupac, who recorded one of the most heartwarming, memorable raps ever, a sweet tribute to his mother called "Dear Mama." Then Tupac gets sent up the river for his role in the gang rape of one of his female fans— a woman, just like his mama.

Gangsta rappers claim their music unifies the black masses, yet they stage those black-on-black bicoastal wars, fiercely protecting turf that the white man owns; they claim their rhymes raise consciousness about white oppression, yet they conspire with that same white man to bring back blaxploitation in another form. Watching some rappers run down their programs on videos, it's clear that despite all their swaggering boasts about wanting to be free from the Man, they crave nothing more than the freedom to be *just like him.* As an artist friend, a guy named Mike Harris, observed, "The brothers who are rapping about being revolutionaries are talking about driving a Lexus all the time."

Bluntly put, some gangsta rappers are no more than jive-ass hypocrites. In that sense, they're no better than the drug dealer, the pimp—or the wicked white man who earns his riches exploiting blacks.

When confronted with their contradictions, some rappers play it dumb. As Snoop Doggy Dogg once suggested in an interview, they claim they don't know any better—nobody has pulled their coats to how their messages influence young blacks.

Others, however, come clean about how they really feel. In the words of Tha Dogg Pound, "Real niggas don't give a fuck." Translated, that means the ruthless brand of capitalism they embrace dictates that the effect of their music on black communities is far less important than "gettin' paid." And that's one reason why gangsta rappers strongly defend their genre. It's a livelihood, and for gangsta rappers it's a sweet one at that. I mean, where else can you get paid millions for taking the ugliest, most low-life ideas that come to mind and making them rhyme? Where else can you be rewarded with money and fame for wallowing, knee-deep, in ignorance?

Despite all their glaring contradictions, gangsta rappers, with their fearless image, still inspire young, impressionable blacks to look to them as the heroes to emulate. And why not? Hero-worship and fantasy are obsessions with young men of all races. The fantasy of heroism is what inspired Japanese kamikaze pilots to fly head-on into ships during World War II; the fantasy of heroism drives young Muslim fundamentalists to volunteer for suicide bombings of their enemies; likewise, the fantasy of distorted bravery, glamorized in gangsta-rap videos and lyrics, leads some young blacks to think it's admirable, that it's dope, to fight the wrong wars for the wrong causes, that it's a noble thing to die an ignoble death.

Nobody fantasizes more than young black men. When you live in a world that works diligently to limit your hopes, reality is often too much to bear. Because they're largely invisible, black males fantasize obsessively about reaching stations in life that they think will raise their profiles and win them the world's acknowledgment. Because they feel powerless, they're consumed with the symbols of power—gangstas, guns, and shoot-'em-ups. So they tune in to the music and imagine themselves as black godfathers and black Al Capones.

And sadly, some actually get up the nerve to act out those roles. They spray gunfire, as a fourteen-year-old did at a crowded D.C. swimming pool one summer, or they gun folks down, like the men in New Orleans whose stray bullets, fired near a well-populated playground, killed a young girl.

It's fantasy, and too often reality for these young bloods doesn't kick in until the handcuffs get slapped on and the charges are read, just as it happened to me.

I was barely out of high school when I shot that dude. When a policeman told my stepfather and me that the guy might die, I became confused and got stuck in the weirdest il-logic: It was clear that if he died, I'd be charged with homi-cide. Yet I would've denied to the hilt that I was a murderer.

If I was seemingly prepared to take somebody's life, why wasn't I prepared to accept the consequences of my actions or concede to being branded a killer? Because on some level, I was certain that the person who shot that guy wasn't really me—it was some gangster I'd *thought* I wanted to be. I'd been fantasizing, and fantasies don't deal with real consequences.

If asked, I could never have *really* explained why I shot that dude. Young and immature, I was completely unaware of the forces driving me. Likewise, many young killers today can't tell you why they did what they did. And when they do try to explain, it becomes even clearer that they don't have a clue.

I often think about these things when I hear of senseless crimes taking young people's lives. I wonder what the assailants might have been fantasizing about. Like the teenager who gunned down a man at a red light because he didn't like the reggae music playing in the man's car.

When I look at the faces of these juvenile assailants during their televised arrests, the first thing I see is the confusion in their eyes when they're being handcuffed by the police and led away. At those moments, they've been jarred and given a serious reality check. They're no longer Ice Cube talking trash or Scarface bragging about his AK-47. They're like what I was: one minute, a swaggering *Godfather* wanna-be; the next minute, a scared, mixed-up teen facing felony charges more serious than I could comprehend.

What all this says to me is that while we've been looking for complex social explanations for the frightening surge in violence afflicting our young, one clue may be right under our noses—and in our ears.

When I think about the insanity of gangsta rap and consider its powerful influence on our young, I'm haunted by the feeling that for African Americans, time is running out. When this party is over years from now, when we look back on these times, we're going to have to answer for why we didn't rescue our children from themselves.

As people whose young are bearing the brunt of the murder and the mayhem, older black Americans should have moved decisively to stop it by now. It's a wonder we haven't cranked up the forces we mobilized in the 1960s, when white police, dogs, and hoses were our most immediate threat.

A handful of black activists, such as C. DeLores Tucker and the Reverend Calvin Butts in New York, have come out strong with consistent attacks against negative rap. But for the most part, black leaders have done little more than mourn the steady, violent passing of this generation's young.

It's not that blacks don't care about what's going on; actually, everybody's shocked and alarmed. But we've been hobbled by several factors that have stumped our collective logic and made us second-guess our simple common sense. For one thing, like everybody else, blacks have been reluctant to campaign to rein in negative rap because of a concern about offending artists' rights to free speech. For another thing, gangsta rap has persisted unchecked because many parents simply are not tuned in. Among older adults, some find rap so irritating that they don't bother to sit down and actually listen to the negative messages their children take in every day.

Finally, gangsta rap has gone unchallenged largely because many blacks are more comfortable confronting external problems. In the civil rights struggle, it was clear we were taking on outside institutions. And if there was some doubt about exactly which institutions we were up against, we at least knew who the enemy was. But today, it's an internal war in which the enemy keeps changing its face. The bad guys used to be white, and some wore sheets and hoods. Now, many are black, and some *are* hoods.

Because the hip-hop movement is so totally black, this is not a battle that whites can get into. If whites got involved in debates about negative rap, the discussion would quickly become sidetracked by issues of race. (That's why Bill Bennett looks and sounds so out of place when he jumps into press conferences with C. DeLores Tucker.)

No, this is a matter for blacks to resolve. It's an in-your-face crisis that comes down to this: In light of the sharp rise in both the number of murders committed by young black men and the number of young black men murdered by their peers, African-American adults must confront the ways in which we're hurting ourselves.

It's obvious that this new reality we face requires an inward approach that may compel us to confront defiant rappers themselves. But it must be done. "We don't have control of our community because we don't have the courage to confront the young people," Chuck D said to me. "You have a lot of black adults who are straight-out afraid of young people, so young people feel they've got more power than the adults. . . . We really need black adults in the community to do something rather than stand back and be spectators."

There's a lot that black adults can do to take more aggressive stands against negative rap. They can launch national boycotts of recording companies and TV and radio stations that put that garbage on the air. They can make everybody accountable, from the black artists who write the songs to the white executives who produce and distribute the music.

Those approaches might help to some degree, but by far the most effective way to deal with gangsta rap is self-censorship. There are indications that within the hip-hop community, pressure for that to happen is building. Among some rappers, there's talk of holding a rap summit, where industry leaders will come together and brainstorm to find ways to use the music for positive purposes. In recent months, some influential names in rap—among them Dr. Dre and Puffy Combs—have announced intentions to rethink their roles. And surprisingly, the cover of a recent issue of *Vibe,* a magazine that chronicles hip-hop, challenged its readers to acknowledge what many of them have denied until now: "The poisonous atmosphere pervading hip hop has claimed its latest victim with the murder of the Notorious B.I.G. All of us in the hip hop community must now come together and take responsibility for ourselves and each other, for our music and our culture—or risk self-destruction."

Ultimately, there's only one sure way to end the ugliness reflected in gangsta rap: Help change the grotesque universe the gangsta rappers sing about. Offer a world so wondrous that it alters their jagged vision of life. That would transform the music and alter the images our children take in. And maybe it would give them something better than violence and abuse to fantasize about.

Portions of this essay have appeared, in a far different form, in The Washington Post *and* Reader's Digest.

THE AMERICAN DREAM

5

THE FATHER OF
OUR COUNTRY

The tour guide stood on the neatly trimmed lawn of the historic Mount Vernon plantation, home of George Washington, the first president of these United States.

Before leading our group through the portion of the tour that covers slave life at Mount Vernon, the guide, Gladys Quander Tancil, asked, "Are there any questions?"

I raised my hand. "Did George Washington have children by any slaves?"

All but four of the forty or so people in the tour group were white. When I posed that question, everybody looked at me.

Mrs. Tancil paused, then raised her eyebrows slightly beneath the straw hat cocked smartly at a slight angle on her head. "The people who run Mount Vernon say he couldn't have children. His wife, Martha, was a widow. She already had two children when they got married."

I never was much on history, but this was heavy stuff, especially considering that there's a black woman living less than three miles from Mount Vernon who claims she's a descendant of George Washington. And especially since there are more black folks scattered in other parts of the country who claim the same thing. It sort of suggests that George was something of a colonial pimp, a gigolo in a powdered wig. It certainly gives new meaning to the description of old George as "the father of our country."

Although he's been dead nearly two hundred years, George Washington is still very relevant now. There's an intimate connection in the mythology surrounding Revolutionary War–era white men like him and the strained race relations in America today. When conservatives such as Rush Limbaugh speak sanctimoniously about "family values," they often cite the white Founding Fathers as the perfect models for all that is good and right. When Newt Gingrich and the boys on Capitol Hill rail against men who fail to take responsibility for their children, they aren't talking at all about white men like them. They're alluding specifically to black males.

I once wondered how those politicians, and whites in general, got such a smug sense of superiority. Visiting Mount

Vernon helped me understand more clearly how the process works. Going there helps you see how the facts—especially as they relate to the behaviors of white men and black men—get twisted so expertly and so completely that, for most ordinary folks, the truth is nowhere to be found.

You see, Mount Vernon is more than just an innocent tourist attraction or a harmless history lesson. It's a propaganda machine. It's one of the many symbols used by the establishment—from the birth of our nation right on up until today—to preserve and promote the cherished myth of the Great White Man.

Located in northern Virginia, right near the line where Virginia and Maryland meet, Mount Vernon is billed as "the nation's most visited historic home." It's open every day, year-round, including holidays, to make sure everybody has access to the myth. More than a million people a year pay about eight dollars to get in, wander the vast grounds, and take in fables about Washington's "heroic" life.

After passing through the entrance of Mount Vernon, you enter a big tent, take a seat on a bench, and watch a thirty-minute videotape called *The Life of George Washington*. The film's narrator says, "Washington's parents taught him the value of honesty and integrity, and these became the guiding principles of his life. He was fair and honest to a fault."

After the film, you move on to Washington's home, a grand

old mansion where other tour guides give you more Yankee-Doodle-Dandy mythology about George. In the home, you see where Washington lived and worked, and many of his and Martha Washington's household possessions are on exhibit there.

The slave tour is separate from the main one. It was started about three years ago after some African Americans pressured Mount Vernon to acknowledge that blacks at least helped keep the place running during Washington's time.

Mrs. Tancil, the woman conducting the tour, said her Mount Vernon bosses do admit that slave life was "depressing." They urged her to make her presentation "lively," so she spends a good bit of the tour discussing her own slave heritage, showing off Washington's garden and stuff like that. Still, the seventy-six-year-old Tancil, whose grandfather was a slave, makes it clear that she's not as taken in by George Washington as are some of her white colleagues. "Some people ask, 'Well, what kind of slave master was he?' " she told the group. Then, with a frown, she said matter-of-factly, "We'd rate him average—average meaning he wasn't that bad and wasn't that good."

Her tour takes you by the slave quarters, a one-story brick building about the size of a one-car garage. You get to see how good old George Washington stacked bunk beds tightly around the walls inside the quarters to cram in as many slaves as possible. Outside, Mrs. Tancil waves her hand toward a tiny patch of ground and says, "This is where the slave children played."

The brief tour is part of an effort to gloss over the "high points" of slave life on Washington's plantation. And the literature handed out at Mount Vernon attempts to do more of the same. "For entertainment at the end of a long day of work, they sometimes played music and sang," says one pamphlet. Above those words is a sketch of a black man sitting in a chair, singing, clapping his hands, and stomping his feet. (Now we know why some white folks still have the mistaken impression that slaves were happy in their bondage.)

Of course, the tour and all the literature conveniently overlook the contradictions in George Washington's life. For instance, they boast a lot about his heroics as a general in the Revolutionary War. It's true that he was a great general. But the literature says nothing about the hypocrisy of this Founding Father fighting to free America from British tyranny while holding 314 black people as slaves.

The literature handed out at Mount Vernon attempts to counteract that contradiction by implying that, by colonial standards, George was a progressive, a liberal who was ahead of his time. "By the end of his life Washington realized that slavery was wrong and freed his slaves," explains one of the handouts. The truth is, he stipulated in his will that his slaves could be freed *after* he and his wife died—in other words, when they didn't need them anymore.

On the Mount Vernon tour you learn as much about our first president from the things that are *not* said about him as by what is expressed. They are what Judith Saunders-Burton calls the "lies of omission." A retired reading specialist who lives in the Mount Vernon district, Saunders-Burton is a black woman who grew up hearing tales about her great-great-great-grandfather, a man named West Ford. Ford is not named in any of the Mount Vernon literature or mentioned during tour presentations. But according to Saunders-Burton's oral family history, he was the black son of George Washington and a slave named Venus, who was owned by Washington's brother, John Augustine.

In her 1986 doctoral thesis at Vanderbilt University, Saunders-Burton traced her ancestry to Ford, who is believed to have been born in 1784 or 1785. "Publicly," West Ford is considered the son of George Washington's nephew, Bushrod. But he is said to have borne a resemblance to George, and one Mount Vernon historian acknowledged that among Washington's family, "there seemed to have been some kind of special feeling" for West Ford. Saunders-Burton in her dissertation pointed out that "West Ford was treated as a family member by the Washingtons. He owned his own home, while others of his race lived in slave quarters. He attended church with the Washingtons, went game hunting with them, and traveled in their company. . . . West Ford's children were educated in the estate schoolhouse along with the Washington children," even though it was illegal to teach blacks to read and write.

One part of the oral history told by other descendants of West Ford states that when Washington became president, he distanced himself from Ford, apparently to avoid the potential public embarrassment that the association would cause.

When Washington died in 1799, West Ford was about fifteen. After Ford turned twenty-one, he was freed by the Washington family and given more than one hundred acres of family land near Mount Vernon, an extraordinary act of generosity toward a black man for that time. He sold the land, then bought other property, which became a settlement for free blacks in an area near Mount Vernon called Gum Springs.

A group known as the Mount Vernon Ladies Association took over as caretakers of Washington's estate in 1858. In 1863, when West Ford had grown old and sickly, the association had him brought back to Mount Vernon to die. Saunders-Burton pointed out in her thesis that in a June 1863 letter to the association's founder, a secretary named Sarah Tracey illustrates that whites regarded West Ford more like a dignitary than a black ex-slave:

We have had old West Ford brought here. Mr. Herbert and myself went to see him Sunday and found him very feeble; and fearing all excitement might hurt him, we have had him brought here, where we could take better care of him. I felt it was our duty to see that he should want for nothing in his old age.

Saunders-Burton said her uncle, who worked at Mount Vernon in the 1950s, claims to have seen a diary naming other children fathered by Washington. When someone discovered him reading it, they confiscated the diary and it was never seen again.

Saunders-Burton gathered most of her information from census and land records, wills, court documents, and archives, but much of it was gleaned from oral history and "circumstantial proof."

But white folks generally don't give much credence to things that aren't documented. So when Saunders-Burton took her information to members of the Mount Vernon Ladies Association, they disputed her claims. "They told me that George Washington had very high standards and that he did not bed down with any slaves. I told them that George Washington did the same as his peers. All of them had slave women.

"The ladies were very upset. They will not allow you to mar George Washington's name at Mount Vernon."

After news of her thesis was published in several newspapers and magazines, Saunders-Burton received telephone calls from other blacks in Colorado, Illinois, and Virginia who said they also were descendants of George Washington. One of those calls came from Linda Bryant, who lives with her family in Aurora, Colorado. West Ford had several children. Two of his sons are the great-great-grandfathers of Saunders-Burton and Bryant, meaning these women are cousins.

The two branches of the family had separated and lost contact years earlier, as some family members passed for white in an attempt to make life easier for themselves. Linda Bryant, who is very fair-skinned, didn't know Judith Saunders-Burton until she read about her dissertation. The amazing thing is that they discovered that, without knowing each other, they had exactly the same accounts of their family heritage. "When she told us her story and we compared our notes, we realized that we really had a good oral story," said Bryant.

Bryant said her mother, who is now eighty, taught her children about the family history. West Ford's mother, the slave Venus, made her son promise to keep the story alive by passing it down through subsequent generations.

Like Saunders-Burton, Bryant contacted the Mount Vernon Ladies Association with her claims. The ladies reiterated the point that Washington's legendary integrity would not have permitted him to be unfaithful. And she was also told that Washington had smallpox, a condition that most likely would have rendered him unable to have children. "I don't care what the Mount Vernon ladies say," Bryant told me. "All of the contemporary men of those days, from Thomas Jefferson to Ben Franklin to Patrick Henry, fathered black children. Men are men. They all were doing it. Why wouldn't George Washington do it too?"

Bryant said her family is willing to submit to DNA tests to prove they're Washington's kin, but they would need to find West Ford's grave to do that. Ford's bone fragments or hair could be matched with still-existing locks of hair from George Washington to determine paternity. Oddly, West Ford's body is missing. The Mount Vernon ladies claim they're not sure where he's buried. They say he might have been buried in a slave graveyard filled with unmarked graves—even though he was a free man when he died.

Bryant suspects that the Mount Vernon Ladies Association orchestrated a cover-up to protect Washington's good name. "If they believed it was important to get [West Ford] and bring him back to Mount Vernon before he died, why would they put him in an unmarked mass grave?"

Bryant and her sister, Janet Allen, an Illinois resident who actually bears a strong resemblance to George Washington, are working on a book about their family heritage. "We're gonna tell it," Bryant said. "We're not trying to do anything to mar George Washington's name and what he stood for, but we want the validation and the vindication to come out. . . . We know who we are. It's not that many generations off."

Whether Washington was unfaithful or not, one thing is clear: Since colonial times, it was a widespread practice among white men to take indecent liberties with black slave women. That means that in addition to being among the first settlers in America, colonial white men were the first real motherfuckers this country has ever known.

Yet it's black males—not white men—who contend with the notion that they have an almost uncontrollable lust for women of another race. You'd think that the history of George Washington and all his compatriots would counteract this enduring stereotype. After all, the physical evidence in America—black people in all their various shades—suggests that white men historically have had a strong appetite for black women.

But you don't get that part of the story on Mount Vernon tours or in our history books. Instead, you get a sanitized version of what went down. You get layers upon layers of B.S. about our forefathers' nobility, about their proud legacy as soldiers, explorers, and family men. It all demonstrates that white historians have given in to a kind of selective amnesia. Using this country's museums and history books, they've taken behaviors that are characteristic of white men and created the perception that such conduct is exclusive to—or more typical of—black males. It amounts to a perceptual sleight-of-hand; it's revisionist history at its very best.

I think that's why most efforts to improve race relations in this country are doomed to fail. Those efforts don't work, primarily because no one requires whites to do their history homework and because America's leaders rarely challenge whites to confront the truth.

In conversations with whites, I'm often amazed at their inability—or unwillingness—to extrapolate about racial matters. Many of the most educated whites I know seem reluctant to connect the dots that link past history to today's reality. I think that's because they've bought into this partial, misleading mythology.

In a very real sense, misleading history has victimized whites as much as anyone else. The myth of the Great White Man has been passed through generations, so that most white people today actually believe the hype. Using the likes of men such as "honest" George Washington as their models, whites today seem to regard themselves as the standard-bearers of values and morality. It's no wonder that their solution to racial problems is to have everyone else learn to be more like them.

Where the legacy of slavery is concerned, many whites also tend to downplay the connection between then and now. They assess current events as if they happened in some historical void. The historical connection is important to recognize because it provides context for understanding behaviors today.

Take, for instance, the debate about black men and illegitimate births. In truth, white men have fathered almost an entire race of people without claiming their children. African Americans, after all, evolved largely from whites like George Washington who were deadbeat dads. That means that colonial white men handed down the legacy of illegitimate white *and* black births that plague this country today.

Gladys Quander Tancil, the Mount Vernon tour guide whose grandfather was a slave, is a living link to the days when black men were prevented by law from being real fathers to their children. It's safe to assume that her grandfather could not teach his sons to be fathers and that they, in turn, could not pass along valuable fathering lessons to their sons. As Linda Bryant said, "It's not that many generations off."

But the popular public perception is that, more than any

other group, black men don't assume responsibility for the children they bring into the world. That stereotype is so deeply ingrained that even some miseducated black people are convinced it's true.

For every one myth about Great White Men such as George Washington (everybody knows the story about the cherry tree), it's as if there are two negative stereotypes about black males. It might not be so bad if the stereotypes were harmless. But they're repeated so often that they soak into the American psyche and take on a life of their own.

One effect of the stereotypes is that, among blacks, they result in a kind of internalized self-hatred. Many blacks hate themselves as much as racist whites hate them. Black-on-black violence is proof of that. The more obvious impact, though, is that those stereotypes, spoken as fact, lead to hostile racial attitudes toward blacks in general. Politicians, in their zeal to appease disgruntled white constituents, actually use those stereotypes as a basis for shaping public policies that affect people's lives.

Consider, for example, the prevailing notion that blacks are lazy people who prefer government handouts to honest jobs. That myth ignores the fact that the institution of slavery itself was rooted in white laziness. It was based on whites' insistence that someone else do their work for *them*—for three hundred years without being paid a single dime.

Still, the public perception now is as it's always been—that blacks, not whites, have an aversion to work. Public opinion polls show that most whites today believe blacks constitute the majority of people on welfare. Actually, there are more whites than blacks on welfare. Yet the hostile welfare policies that have come down from politicians recently stemmed largely from whites' perceptions about blacks' unwillingness to work.

The distortion of history and the wholesale use of stereotypes has a terrible effect on African Americans. Among many of us, there's a deep-seated resentment toward America, and that resentment threatens to boil over, especially when we see self-righteous conservatives using their forefathers' morality as a basis to criticize blacks. For many blacks, the widespread use of stereotypes against them is concrete proof that the promise of American equality is an outright lie. The feeling is this: How can you ever expect fair treatment from people whose self-perception is rooted on lofty myths and whose opinion of you is based on distorted facts?

Several years ago, when the movie director Oliver Stone made *JFK,* a film about the Kennedy assassination, critics accused him of distorting history. His response applies to all of America: "We are the children of distorted history."

If this country is to move beyond race, first and foremost, we need to learn the facts about our shared past. Such an examination might require us to revise America's museums and history books and throw away the mythology that serves as the foundation of white supremacy.

There's no better place to start than by telling the truth about the father of our country on the Mount Vernon tour and including the details about George Washington's black descendants.

6

OLD TOWN: THE NEGRO PROBLEM REVISITED

If you want a glimpse of what's *really* happening with race relations in this country, go on over to Old Town in Alexandria,
Virginia, and check out the scene. There's a street there—
North Fairfax Street—that embodies white America's greatest hopes and, at the same time, symbolizes black folks'
deepest frustrations. On one side of North Fairfax Street is an
old, decaying, mostly black public-housing project where
rents average about two hundred dollars per month. On the
other side of the street are stately, relatively new two-
hundred-thousand-dollar brick townhouses inhabited largely
by whites.

Although white people generally do their absolute best to

live as far away from blacks as possible, it's oddly different in Old Town. White folks are moving onto North Fairfax and other black-populated streets at breakneck speed.

Local white civic leaders will tell you that the influx of whites is part of what helps make Old Town a model of integration, but that's not quite true. The reason for the flood of whites has nothing to do with racial harmony. The truth is it's a gold rush: The blacks have something whites desperately want—prime property located near a "historic" area that overlooks the scenic Potomac River.

The impoverished blacks in the one-hundred-unit project, which is nicknamed the Berg, live just two blocks from the waterfront, where jogging and bike trails have sprung up and where there are pastoral parks and a nice marina that runs out into a river setting as placid as anything you'll ever see.

But space and housing are limited. And because whites want that land so badly, they've come to view the project dwellers, as well as blacks in the area who own their homes, as a problem—as in "the Negro problem." It's a classic illustration of how blacks in America have routinely been perceived since slavery times. Throughout this country, blacks have learned this: When we're regarded as a problem, it's time to watch out. Suffering and pain are on the way.

The blacks in Old Town know that Caucasians would

never move near them without some strong assurances from somebody somewhere that "the Negro problem" will be eliminated in due time. And it's quite apparent, just from passing through, that a grand scheme is under way to do just that.

If all goes according to plans, bulldozers and wrecking balls will eventually take care of the blacks on North Fairfax Street. Even as I write these words, there's a proposal in place to demolish the Berg and move the blacks out—to relocate them, in urban-speak. In addition, black business owners and homeowners also have come under intense pressure from whites to move someplace else.

In the meantime, the city—the establishment, the Man—has taken methodical steps to ensure the protection of white townhouse owners on North Fairfax Street. Their tactics evoke images of South Africa before Nelson Mandela was freed.

For starters, the townhouses on North Fairfax Street are surrounded by a large brick wall—an urbanized fortress, really—that completely shields them from all that annoying poverty across the street. Also, the whites' interests are guarded—mightily—by the local police. Every few minutes— as regularly as guards at an army post—a cop car cruises slowly around the two blocks ringing the townhouses and the housing projects. It's obvious that the lawmen are there to shield whites from any threats, perceived or real, from those desperate niggers who may covet what they have.

The police presence is so strong that Kayna Carter, who lives in the projects, says she feels "imprisoned" in her own neighborhood. Like others, she complains of the frequent "jump outs," when special police squads drive up to blacks in the streets, spring from their cars, and arrest them for even the slightest infractions. "They have police satellite offices, so the police presence shouldn't have to be that strong," Carter said as she sat in her living room one evening. "They're kind of building a case for themselves to justify their long-term goal. They're doing everything possible to put blacks out."

Beyond guarding the sanctity of white life, the establishment's motivation for getting rid of blacks in Old Town is pegged to money. There are precious tourism dollars at stake. Old Town promotes itself as "one of America's oldest port towns," and in 1996 alone tourists spent $316 million in Alexandria on hotels, food, tours, and all that visitors do.

The amazing thing is that if you called the whites of Old Town racists, they'd probably be highly offended. You see, they view themselves as progressives. Largely, they're educated professionals who are civic-minded and health oriented. They're well-read, and they vote. And unlike their standoffish counterparts, who constantly flee farther and farther into the outer reaches of the burbs, they're willing to move into the heart of cities like Alexandria and help sustain the tax base.

Old Town whites will assure you that they're not racist. They'll say they value the "multicultural experience," which for many means a good meal at a Vietnamese, Thai, or soul-food restaurant. When I ask the police about it, a spokesman insists that they "have an excellent relationship with all our citizens." And whites with deep ties to the place, such as Barbara Barton, describe it as "a very amicable racial setup."

"By and large, Alexandria tends to get along. There's nothing overt," said Barton, who works for the Office of Historic Alexandria. "I will say this: If we have tensions, I don't think they're racial as much as economic."

Such an assessment seems far from the view of Old Town blacks, who frequently grumble about "those white people trying to force us out." But whites like Barton have the luxury of believing that everything on the racial front is just la-di-da. That's because they don't sully their hands doing the dirty work of displacing blacks. They have the system to do that for them.

In fairness to them, many Old Town whites probably don't hate blacks or anyone else. But what they often overlook is their utter disregard for black life; their shallow respect, which is tenuous, conditional at best: They value black life, and all other life—until it interferes with what they want. "When they can see that they can get any kind of profit," Kayna Carter said, "they get it, and they don't care who they hurt. . . . It's ugly, what's going on. It's a vicious, vicious cycle."

It's an arrogance that runs so deep it blinds them to the many ways in which they casually trample on other human beings; it's a well-developed, selective naïveté that historically has enabled them to oppress and destroy others, conscience free.

That's why Old Towns everywhere typically have a public pride and a private shame. That's why they often have one history they promote and another history they conceal. For instance, the literature distributed by the Alexandria Convention and Visitors Association will tell you that Old Town was the childhood home of Civil War general Robert E. Lee and that our first president, George Washington, maintained a townhouse there. "Venture south of King Street near the Potomac River and Old Town looks much as it did in the days of our founding fathers," one pamphlet boasts.

The locals will proudly tell you that even during the time of slavery, Old Town was always integrated—sort of. Of course, whites controlled the place, but blacks who worked for them as servants were allowed to live peacefully in neighborhood pockets, mostly down near the waterfront.

What the glossy pamphlets and the proud locals fail to point out is that long before anybody had even heard the term *environmental racism,* it was standard practice in Old Town. The houses near the waterfront, where blacks lived, sat next to smelly old factories and plants that white folks wouldn't dare live near.

Then, in the 1940s, when the city fathers decided to build public housing in the area, they did a predictable thing: They declared "eminent domain," which is a technical term that allows the city to take whatever land it wants from whomever it pleases, so long as it's used for public purposes. So the city took the black folks' homes, demolished them, and built projects like the Berg.

"They gave the blacks what they wanted to give them for their houses," Eudora Lyles, a longtime Old Town resident, told me.

She should know. A white-haired, copper-toned lady who has lived in her home for more than fifty years, Eudora Lyles has spent a lifetime fighting a system that's as well preserved as those old colonial houses Old Town boosters brag about. While raising four children, this widow organized a civic association to battle the powers at city hall.

On a map of Old Town, she showed me where white city fathers throughout the years have relocated black homeowners to make way for various "redevelopment" projects, and she told me how, each time, they left whites' homes in the same areas untouched. "You can see the pattern. Every time they took homes, the blacks were the ones who suffered," she said, her anger growing. "But if your house happened to be on a block where there was *one* white family, it would be spared."

When the city set about gentrifying the area, using the waterfront as a lure, it began by eliminating the unsightly, polluting factories. The next step, Mrs. Lyles says, was to go after the blacks, many of whose homes had been passed down to them over generations dating back to the Civil War. "It was all right for us to be down there when they had a dump and different stinking plants on the waterfront. But when they started upgrading, they wanted to move the blacks out of there."

In the years since then, blacks in Old Town have watched resentfully as whites worked to claim the entire place, using housing-code violations and other convenient tools of the legal system to weed them out.

Margarette Cooper, who has lived with her family in Old Town since the 1950s, can tell you how city officials denied a black friend of hers a permit to build a house on a certain lot, which they said was too small. The friend moved elsewhere. Then, a short time later, the city allowed a white family to build a house on that same forbidden spot. "The house was built in the shape of an L so that it would fit onto the lot," Mrs. Cooper said. "It makes me mad every time I look at that house."

For black homeowners in Old Town, it's not unusual for smiling white strangers to come uninvited, knock at their doors, and outright ask them if they're willing to sell. The whites are betting that they're so hard-pressed for money they'll be forced to cave. Bernard Barron, who has lived on North Alfred Street most of his life, has been bombarded with letters and phone calls from white realtors eager to cash in on the demand for property. "They want to know if I'm willing to sell. . . . I don't respond."

Like Barron, some Old Town blacks, by hook, crook, or determined will, manage to hold on to their homes. Others aren't so lucky or shrewd. Along with the powerless poor, elderly black homeowners are the easiest targets. Living on fixed incomes, many of them can't keep pace with rising taxes and home-repair costs and are forced to sell.

Barron watches as realtors show houses for sale to chipper white couples eager to move onto his street, which is still mostly black. He thinks it's no coincidence that he never sees blacks being shown these homes. "I cannot prove it. It's just a gut feeling. . . . I've not seen four blacks shown these houses."

When all else fails to persuade blacks in Old Town to give

up their homes, downright harassment kicks in. You can see it, especially on the western end of Queen Street, where a cluster of black-owned barbershops and bookstores constitute the bulk of the mom-and-pop black businesses remaining in Old Town. (Some business owners have turned down multimillion-dollar offers for their land.)

Near the intersection of Queen and North Fayette Streets, two white policemen often sit in a cruiser, contemptuously watching the ebb and flow of black life. Farther down the block, an officer on foot patrol scans the area. The strong police presence on Queen Street seems somewhat strange when you consider that in most black areas it's usually hard to get the police to come promptly when you call. But not here. Police are already on the scene, whether you need them or not.

Police Lieutenant John Crawford insists that "there's no racial bias over here. The crime dictates where we go. . . . If you're selling drugs, we're jumping you."

For years, the corner of Queen Street and North Fayette has been a social gathering spot, and it certainly has its share of drunks and druggies hanging out. But some blacks have their own theories about the police's motives for being there.

Guy Boston, a barber on Queen Street, figures it's about short-term containment until "the Negro problem" can be obliterated. He thinks it's about making the black people living there feel so unwelcome that maybe, just maybe, they'll get fed up and leave. "I wasn't born just yesterday!" Boston shouts angrily when asked about the police. "They can't spin me around three times and kick me in my butt and think that I'm so dizzy that I don't know what's going on. . . . The white folks moving in here want all the old elements out."

Glancing toward the corner, where the police cruiser sits, Boston, a tall, wiry, dark-skinned man who sports a derby while he works, rolls his eyes. "It's not that anybody sent for these white folks to come down here. But wherever there's water and a certain atmosphere, that's where they gonna be."

Among older blacks, there's a certain resignation about being driven from Old Town. Like Eudora Lyles, who is seventy-nine, most older blacks—in Old Town and every-where else—have been conditioned to submerge their rage when whites callously push them aside. The elderly are more likely to shrug their shoulders and exclaim, *That's just the way things are.* Even now, with strong convictions about what's going down, Mrs. Lyles is clearly bitter, but she won't dare use that word to describe how she feels. It's no wonder. The huge Bible on her coffee table and the praying hands and portrait of the Reverend Jesse Jackson on the wall in her tiny living room explain her stance. In the black church that nur-tures her, *bitter* is an ugly word. Bitter leads to hatred, and hatred is sin.

Instead of saying she's bitter, Mrs. Lyles, who looks like

everyone's sweet grandmother, prefers to describe her emotions in more acceptable Christian terms: "It hurts to sit back and see these things happening and know that people don't know. I don't understand why people can't see it. I'm saddened," she said as her voice quaked.

Mrs. Lyles is so unsettled about her rage that she even second-guesses her basic instincts about right and wrong. During one of my visits, she shared her ambivalence about the recurring resentment she feels toward Old Town whites. "I have mixed feelings about the fight," she said. "I wonder, is it wrong for them to extend Old Town and have people move in and make it better?"

I tell her what I think: "Yes, it's wrong when you do it at the expense of other people like this."

Gazing through her front window, reflecting for a moment, she turned back to me. "Yeah, that's true. That's true."

Younger blacks are different. Like Guy Boston, this generation's blacks are more likely to trust their instincts and wear their outrage on their sleeves. Their frustration has them restless. They want to do *something*. They want to fight back or raise hell, strike out at the amorphous system converging on them, but they haven't figured out just what to do.

There has been some organized resistance. In 1996, a residents group filed a formal complaint charging that the city has continually discriminated against blacks in its housing policies. Filed by the Alexandria Resident Council, the complaint said the city's housing authority intentionally refused to use federal funds to renovate the Berg, virtually assuring that the complex of two-story brick row houses, built in 1945, would become dilapidated.

Of course, the city's position is that it's doing what's in the best interests of the blacks. They've promised that some of the displaced blacks will be allowed to move back into newer, higher-priced townhouses. As for the others, the city plans to give them vouchers so they can rent houses at "scattered sites" throughout Alexandria. But nobody, at least none of the blacks I talked to, believes that plan will benefit anyone but the white folks who want to acquire land to build new, expensive housing for more white folks to move into.

The fight against the white incursion has been rather limited, though. In large part, area blacks lack the sophistication needed to effectively battle city hall. For Eudora Lyles, the struggle has been lonely and frustrating. "The public-housing tenants are scared. No matter who tries to help them, they can't get the kind of cooperation they need."

And the black homeowners?

"Let me tell you about our people," she said angrily. "We don't understand the workings of the city insofar as taxes and ordinances and things. I tried to get them involved in the zoning and other matters, and they had their choir meetings and their usher board meetings to go to. A lot of them would not pull in and be interested because they're not trained that way. . . . Unless we understand how these things affect our community, we can't protect ourselves."

Despite the feeble resistance to the white takeover of black Old Town, many blacks are braced for the inevitable. Lillian Patterson, who works at a local black museum, lamented one day how the neighborhood she grew up in is being transformed before her eyes. "There isn't a physical black community anywhere anymore. There aren't two blocks where there are just blacks."

Cruising through Old Town, you can actually see the grand American dreamscape whites are creating for themselves. You can see it on Eudora Lyles's street, where white contractors hammer away, refurbishing old homes, many of which were once owned by blacks. FOR SALE signs adorn the tiny front yards of other houses along the block, foreshadowing what's to come.

You can also see it in such places as the Old Town business district, only several blocks from the Berg. The business area is a bustling scene where some whites stroll easily in and out of antique shops, art galleries, and gourmet restaurants while others sit at sidewalk cafés and sip Chablis—even in the cold or the drizzling rain. (They're so in love with the fucking dream that they won't even allow the *weather* to interfere.)

The business district is filled with quaint gift and specialty shops. Like Old Town itself, these shops reek of unabashed patriotism and breezy hypocrisy. One shop is even named America. It features an array of patriotic merchandise in red, white, and blue. There's a life-size poster of Hillary Rodham Clinton and, of course, pictures of George Washington everywhere. And flags. American flags of all sizes and a few Confederate ones, too. You can even buy Confederate swimming trunks that glow in the dark!

The people who wander by have a sameness about them, like the women who jaunt down sidewalks swigging Evian water and pushing strollers carrying red-cheeked, contented-looking babies. There are black women pushing strollers, too—they're domestics entertaining the white people's babies they care for during the day.

And lots of the folks who amble through Old Town carry cameras. For them, life is a succession of Kodak moments, and city officials certainly don't want black folks to spoil the view.

It doesn't take a psychic to figure out what Old Town is shaping up to be. Standing on his front porch on a sunny day, Bernard Barron scanned the street that was once filled with blacks. "This block is changing," he said. "This area is becoming more and more like Georgetown."

Barron didn't have to say more than that. Georgetown, located on the other side of the Potomac, in Washington, D.C., is one of the premier Old Towns in America. Years ago, before Franklin D. Roosevelt's first term, Georgetown was a neighborhood that was black owned and run. (You wouldn't know that now if you saw the place.) When whites decided they wanted it, they moved in, raised taxes, and quietly drove blacks out. Now they sashay through Georgetown—fashionable Georgetown, it's often called—like it's always been theirs.

Like Old Town, Georgetown has a strong police presence. Although crime there is relatively low, the cops are there in force, often neglecting poorer, more crime-ridden parts of the city, where they're needed most.

As an added measure, some well-to-do Georgetown residents have their own private cops to patrol their streets. On M Street and Wisconsin Avenue, the main shopping strip, business owners bring in black security guards and post them, like sentries, at their stores' entrances.

When I walk into Georgetown stores, security guards converge on me quickly, as if I'm trespassing on private property. I get the message: Blacks aren't welcome there at all.

In most larger American cities—such as Philadelphia, Chicago, Baltimore, and Detroit—there are variations of Old Town. Maybe there's one near you. These are the chic sections of the cities, created as playgrounds for upwardly mobile whites, those health-club yuppies who move there to nurture fairy-tale fantasies of a booming America that caters *solely* to them.

These are trendy districts that often have cobblestone streets and restored historic homes replete with wrought-iron gates—all features that nourish their residents' obsessive yearning to relive their "glorious" past.

"Nostalgia is what they want," the singer Gil Scott-Heron once observed. "They wanna go back. They wanna go *way* back, to a time when television was in black and white—and so was everything else."

Old Towns are usually known for their funky French, Italian, and other eateries. They're also known for their high-fashion clothiers and their live entertainment (preferably soul and jazz—it makes the tourists feel hip).

On any given day or night, the sidewalks of America's Old Towns are filled to the brim, mostly with white people. You see them wandering in crowded herds on the main drag. Especially on weekends, you see them moving casually about in their Gap jeans, Polo shirts, and Ray•Ban shades. They stroll hand in hand, browsing in store windows and ducking playfully into swank restaurants along the busy strip.

Except for the handful of beggars who are sometimes tolerated because their presence adds a certain diversity to the scene, poor people don't even bother much going there. They know the Old Towns of America are reserved for faithful voters and moneyed taxpayers.

For affluent whites and wanna-bes, life in Old Town is the hippest version of the American dream. That dream—although a little harder to come by these days—is still a real possibility within their grasp.

For blacks, it's still mostly a hallucination. It's a hoax that keeps them running in frustrated circles, like a dog chasing its tail.

Like the blacks in Alexandria—and in Old Towns everywhere—African Americans see their access to the dream perpetually blocked by a brutal contradiction that at times drives them truly mad. The contradiction is this: Whites pretend to embrace the notion of equal opportunity as part of the dream, but at the same time, whites cannot—they *will not*—tolerate an America where that's literally true. Even some of the most well intentioned whites—those whose rhetoric suggests they want the dream to be accessible to everyone—don't really intend for it to work across the board.

It's the contradiction of white supremacy. Whites profess to believe in the equality of the races, but in reality they believe more firmly in the superiority of their own race. Only southern crackers, Klansmen, and members of other "fringe" groups openly admit that. But on some level, most so-called progressive whites, in Old Towns and everywhere else, believe it, too. *Nostalgia is what they want.*

Whether they admit it or even think about it, I believe that whites certainly know the truth: that although they may not be guilty themselves, they still benefit, directly or indirectly, from blacks' afflictions.

In that way, Old Towns symbolize the American way: America *takes* what it wants. Of course, that's not in keeping with the myth of this country, but it certainly reflects its practice—here and throughout the world.

When white folks "discovered" America, it already belonged to somebody else. Whites decided they wanted it, so they took it. Now they feel perfectly justified in treating everyone else like intruders. *America,* they shout pompously, *love it, or leave it.*

And when blacks protest, they somehow come to be regarded as a problem—the Negro problem.

Frederick Douglass had it right, though. He said, "There is no Negro problem. The problem is whether the American people have loyalty enough, honor enough, patriotism enough, to live up to their own Constitution."

When I think of how the Old Towns of America are established—often at the expense of people who are pushed, cajoled, enticed, or otherwise forced to abandon their homes to make way for whites, I am reminded of an incident that happened several years ago at a Shoney's restaurant in North Carolina. While heading to the salad bar, I heard a commotion. When I moved closer, I saw a thirtyish black man yelling at a scruffy white guy. It seems that the white man had shoved an elderly black man, who was standing in line in front of him. The younger black, seeing the insult, intervened in his elder's behalf. I got there just in time to hear the redneck angrily justify his rudeness. "He was in my way!" he snarled, pointing at the old man.

The white man's audacity infuriated the brother. Stepping closer, he shouted, "He was in your way? Your way? Motherfucka, you ain't *got* no way!"

The old man seemed embarrassed by it all. He stood quietly, watching the tension between the two young hotheads escalate. At some point, the brother stepped even closer to the white man—he got to within an inch of his nose, daring him to make a move. And as he did that, I instinctively slipped behind the redneck, readying my plate, which I fully intended to crash upside his head.

I didn't know the old black man any more than I knew the brother defending him—we were all strangers. But I was fairly certain that we shared some common experiences: If they live long enough, most blacks experience being deemed a problem because some white person or persons decide that we're in their way.

That realization was enough to make that brother and me want to take out the wrath of slavery on that redneck—not only for hassling the elderly black but for all the Old Towns, where black life is disrupted or vanquished to accommodate white folks' fancies, for all the times white America has said to blacks, *Step aside. You're in my way.*

Apparently sensing what he was up against, the white boy sensibly backed down, and the elderly black man went on to prepare his plate.

For the younger black dude and me, that moment represented a rare, if symbolic, triumph over white arrogance. But it also represented a sad kind of truth: that countless small and large offenses are routinely committed against blacks who never have anyone to speak up in their behalf. There's so much pain nonchalantly inflicted merely because black folks are in whites' "way."

So it is with Old Town.

Years from now, when the deal is done, Old Town, Alexandria, will be just like Georgetown—expensive, elitist, and white. The project dwellers will have packed their few possessions and memories and left, and the black homeowners will have died off or given in to the persistent pressure to sell. And if they should return to visit Old Town, they won't be welcome—unless they're there to wait tables or deliver goods. They'll be looked on as intruders, regarded suspiciously in the community they once called home.

7

FAKING THE FUNK: THE MIDDLE-CLASS BLACK FOLKS OF PRINCE GEORGES COUNTY

When the sun is out and the weather is nice, about fifteen young bloods sometimes gather on the corner of Lake Arbor Way and Winged Foot Drive. Maybe in their late teens, they chill on that spot, rap casually, and slyly pass forty-ounce bottles of brew from hand to hand.

Of course, they sport the popular gangsta look and wear the standard street gear: knit skullcaps pulled over their shaved heads; bulky, unlaced brogans; and baggy sweatshirts flung over blue jeans that ride low—*real low*—on their butts.

In dress and manner, they could pass for a typical crew of young hustlers in Washington, D.C. And as you drive by, they even eye you warily, like leery drug dealers scoping for the

Man. But cruising through there, you're struck by the realization that something's wrong with this picture. There's a major contradiction here. There's something that, well, just doesn't seem to make sense.

The discrepancy begins with the setting: The backdrop for the fellas is not boarded-up tenements, graffiti-marked walls, and urban blight. The backdrop is $250,000 homes with manicured lawns—houses that are sprinkled around a sprawling, well-tended community golf course and near jogging trails that circle a scenic, man-made lake.

In other words, this is not the rugged Chocolate City, where the gang bangers rule. This is Prince Georges County, a serene suburb of Washington. And the dudes hanging on the corner aren't desperate hoods trying to survive a hardscrabble life; they're middle-class black kids with braces on their teeth. They're wanna-bes who are just acting out, pretending to be the gritty street warriors they see in D.C.

If you think *they're* a little confused, you should see their parents.

Their parents are the professional and business people who help make Prince Georges the richest majority-black county in the United States. By practically every barometer—income, education, and so on—used by our "social experts," they're the black crème de la crème. But like their children, they seem to be caught up in a bizarre identity crisis of some sort. And just like their offspring, their struggle is sometimes a pathetic sight.

In the normal scheme of things, the middle-class black people of Prince Georges County (everyone calls it P.G. for short) wouldn't be particularly noteworthy. In most ways, they're just typical Americans—or they're what we tend to think average Americans are: They're hardworking, honest folks who want the best for themselves and their families. They're good people—the kind of black folks that whites seem to get little exposure to.

But they are also something else. They are black America's crystal ball: Hailed by the media as a "national showcase for black achievement," P.G. is a scale model of what *is* and *is not* happening among the most promising African Americans in this splintered land. And the goings-on of brothers and sisters there offer some clues about the future, especially for the black poor, who are catching hell.

The middle-class blacks of Prince Georges County symbolize our greatest hope. They're part of a spontaneous, quietly budding movement that seems to be catching on everywhere. In suburbs surrounding cities such as Atlanta, Philadelphia, and Chicago, the movement consists of upwardly mobile blacks who have broken from the pattern of following white folks wherever they settle. Instead, these blacks have made a conscious decision to live among their own.

Unlike the movements of the past, which were in-your-face and on the streets, this one is more subtle and more instinctive. In fact, it's so low-key that you can become a part of it without even realizing it.

It happened that way for me several years ago, when my teenage son came to live with me in D.C. With my son so close by, the city worried me as never before: Too many people have become casualties of the crack epidemic or the out-of-control gangsterism that's made Washington seem like a war zone. So we did what lots of black folks have done: We left.

First, we moved in with my sister-in-law in a mostly white Virginia suburb. There, I faced the usual hassles that you encounter when living among whites: suspicious Caucasians whispering concerns to our landlord that we might bring down their property values or break into their houses and rip off their TVs.

Often when I left home for work at *The Washington Post,* I encountered so many wary whites on sidewalks and buses that I often was pissed off by the time I reached the office in downtown D.C. Disgusted, I decided to move someplace else, someplace where I could get away from paranoid whites.

That's when I heard about P.G. I was told that in some parts of the county, blacks had formed enclaves in peaceful communities as nice as you'll find anywhere. I went to a place called Mitchellville, looked around, and bought a townhouse right away.

Before blacks moved there in large numbers, Prince Georges County was one vast cow pasture run by white, beer-bellied good old boys. Blacks began moving in around the 1970s. Two decades later, the county of 750,000 had a black majority. In 1994, blacks showed off their new political might and elected the first black county executive ever to run the place.

Of course, there are working-class and even some poor areas in P.G., just like anywhere else, but the county is known mostly for the large concentration of well-off blacks who have settled there. The community where I now live, known as Lake Arbor, is surrounded by others very much like it—developments called Fort Washington, Kettering, Perrywood. These are sprawling, rustic neighborhoods where the median income is relatively high and the crime is low. A survey found that blacks with college degrees outnumber college-educated whites in P.G. County and that more blacks than whites live in households with earnings above fifty thousand dollars. P.G. has also become a magnet for local black celebrities. For-mer heavyweight champion Riddick Bowe, the writer Marita Golden, and several NBA basketball stars live there.

Any P.G. resident will tell you what it means to feel wel-come in your community. Often, when I step out onto my deck and scan the woodsy landscape that fronts my neighborhood, the tranquillity of the place fills me with a deep sense of racial pride. My euphoria is prompted partly by the atmosphere, which is really nice: The townhouses where I live stand in the shadows of a lake, a golf course, and large houses. But more than that, the good feeling comes from the realization that this may be as close to heaven as I will ever get: I can travel for a couple of miles in any direction and see mostly black folks, mostly *my* people; I can step outdoors without worrying about being insulted by some arrogant white dude who thinks I'm after his wallet; I can stroll through my neighborhood without seeing some old, blue-haired white lady clutching her bags when she sees me. In fact, when I go outdoors, my neighbors are genuinely glad to see me. They wave and say a cheerful hello.

Driving through my neighborhood, you can't help being impressed. And if you're not careful, you can get *really* carried away and interpret the outward appearance of things as a promising sign that we black people are finally pulling ourselves together. As the theme song for the old sitcom *The Jeffersons* went, it looks like "we're movin' on up."

But as the young bloods who hang on that corner demonstrate, things aren't always what they appear to be. The truth is, some blacks in P.G. County are living what one of my neighbors called an illusion of success. Their houses are impressive and their cars look expensive, but few have any real wealth to speak of. Many are not even nigger rich, though some have learned, damned well, to act the part. Although they may *look* as though they have things together, many are just groping in the dark. A schoolteacher who moved there recently from Florida told me, "They seem to have lost their focus. They're just like ostriches with their heads in the sand."

What she meant is that among the "successful" blacks of P.G. and, by extension, middle-class blacks everywhere, many have failed the crucial commitment test: This crowd— my generation of college-trained blacks—came up in the world with some high expectations heaped on them. We are the people expected to form the "talented tenth" that W.E.B. Du Bois imagined; we rode the shoulders of our predecessors, the civil rights protesters who fought, and sometimes sacrificed their lives, to open doors for us. We were expected to use our skills and training to take the black struggle to the next level. For a long time, it was assumed that when we got our chance, we'd figure out a way to reach back and help those poor blacks who were left in the urban trenches to fend for themselves.

But if the prosperous blacks in P.G. County are any indication, the huddled poor masses may just have to wait awhile. The truth is, black America's middle class is a conflicted bunch of people who are still unsure of the power they wield. Right now, they can't save the poor—they're too preoccupied trying to figure out who *they* are.

Despite all the material signs of progress, there's no indication that the middle-class movement will spread beyond the thriving bounds of places like P.G. County and embrace those blacks most in need of our help.

For one thing, there's no concrete game plan at work here. This middle-class movement is not spearheaded by the NAACP or the National Urban League or even by some charismatic leader. There's no indication that the man or woman who will be the next Martin Luther King, Jr., or Malcolm X will spring from this bunch to lead the way. You get the feeling that the college-trained blacks with that kind of potential are too busy hustling the dollar, trying to make partner in some prominent white law firm.

"I think that too many of us are too tied to the system to be effective in the way that Martin and Malcolm were. Martin and Malcolm weren't beholden to the system," noted one friend, a lawyer who also lives in P.G.

The result is that the movement lacks direction. So the black people of Prince Georges County—and middle-class African Americans everywhere—are improvising; they're just taking the black struggle day by day.

As I wonder about my own role in helping the poor, I realize that the main question the black middle class faces is this: Beyond the quest for financial security and personal comfort, what, if anything, are we committed to? It's not that we don't have plenty of good, firsthand reasons to fight for the cause. A *Washington Post* story on the subject said, "Middle-class African Americans are more likely to feel they face racism than working-class and poor blacks. Nearly six in 10 middle-class blacks say they have experienced racism in the past 10 years and six in 10 say that they are concerned that they or a family member will face discrimination in the future."

The writer of the article, Kevin Merida, went on to say, "This unease comes at a time when many high-achieving blacks see their status threatened by corporate and government downsizing and their gains being challenged in the courts, in the political arena and in the theories of conservative scholars. As a result, though they are viewed within their race as having 'made it,' they are drawing closer politically to those who haven't."

Yet middle-class blacks clearly are not drawing closer to the black poor in other ways. Like cats curled up comfortably on a favorite rug, many of them live in what amounts to what the writer Sam Fulwood described as a "self-protective buppie cocoon, separate from poor blacks and all whites."

The blacks in Prince Georges seem to bear that out. If P.G. County is a symbol of success for the black middle class, for the poor it's also a discouraging sign of black flight. Of course, the term *black flight* makes many middle-class blacks cringe. In defense of themselves, some are quick to point out that theirs is not flight in the traditional sense of the word. (Blacks in P.G. want you to know that they're not so much running *from* something as running *to* something.)

Still, many middle-class blacks in P.G., and everywhere else, seem to be nagged by a deep sense of guilt about the notion that they've abandoned the poor. "I shouldn't feel guilty, because I didn't get a free ride," Bravitte Manley, a corporate lawyer, once told me. "But when you see blacks who are hopeless, you feel guilty, and you feel helpless because you don't know how to make the situation better. What most people do is try not to think about it because if you think about it, it's intellectually unjustifiable to say, *So what?*"

The guilt stems from the fact that for many African Americans who have come into their own in recent decades, economic success has been double-edged: It's brought them material comfort, but it's distanced them—physically and emotionally—from those for whom the mainstream remains out of reach.

In response, the so-called black underclass has created a defiant counterculture all its own. It has developed its own language, values, music, and—as ruthless as the drug trade may be—a self-sustaining industry. That counterculture has evolved so swiftly and furiously, and the devastation of poverty and violence in its wake is so far-reaching, that it's left the entire nation dumbfounded. The astonishing murder rate among blacks attests to this.

The result is that now, in the midst of one of the toughest challenges ever to our collective survival, middle-class and poor blacks have become terribly divided. This estrangement has crippled our struggle, which once had unity. "I've been disgusted with myself because I've become very class-conscious and very mainstream," a friend once confessed to me. "I don't feel personal guilt, but I do feel ashamed that many of us who have arrived have not banded together to help the underclass. I struggle with that."

In P.G. County, some folks try to relieve their guilty feelings by taking up social causes. But they don't seem like the kinds of folks who'd actually go to the ghetto and work in the trenches. They're more likely to scribble a check in arm's-length support of some worthy black cause. Or they'll turn to mentoring and other relatively risk-free activities to convince themselves that at least they're doing *something*.

It doesn't help matters that some middle-class blacks secretly relish their buppie status. For such folks, even charity is a status symbol. Jackie Woods, a friend who has lived in Philly, Chicago, and D.C., told me about a gathering she attended that could easily have passed for a scene in a Tom

Wolfe novel: A group of well-to-do blacks got together in an elegant high-rise apartment, drinking wine and nibbling asparagus tips and lobster while planning fund-raisers to help the homeless. "There were twenty-five people in the room, and everybody had on a thousand dollars worth of clothes," she said. "We were talking about helping the homeless, and there wasn't a homeless person in the room."

I truly believe that most middle-class blacks do want to help. Like me, they feel frustrated and so overwhelmed by the complex web of problems facing African Americans that they don't know where to begin. It's also true that virtually every element in America's black communities is pitching in. People in neighborhoods are taking to the streets to help the police fight crime. Civil rights groups are launching public relations campaigns to stop the violence. And churches, as usual, are doing their thing.

One battle cry that you hear more often now is the call for black suburbanites to return and help revive the cities they've abandoned. But the option of returning poses a serious practical problem: At a time when bystanders are often caught in the cross fire of gun battles, most people with a choice are understandably reluctant to place themselves and their families at risk. For many, it's plain foolish to go back when it's clear that the people there are fighting losing battles with drug lords armed with automatic weapons.

The issue of whether or not to return to the city is not just about establishing a physical presence. Unfortunately, some middle-class blacks also consider it necessary to distance themselves totally from the problems confronting us. In action, if not in philosophy, they subscribe to the view of Reverend Ike, the slick-haired, money-loving preacher who says, "The best thing you can do for the poor is not to become one of them."

So some middle-class blacks create their own strange existence, one that leaves them torn between two conflicting worlds: On the one hand, they're disillusioned by the racial realities of America, which hates blacks and the poor; on the other hand, they're still in love with the idea and the hope of achieving white folks' American dream. They're troubled by their loyalty—or lack of it—to less fortunate blacks, and yet for all their striving, for all the effort they've made to live among their own kind, the model of middle-class success that they pattern themselves on is lily-white.

Drive to Mitchellville Plaza, one of the many little shopping centers that have sprung up near upscale P.G. neighborhoods, and you'll see what I mean. You'll catch hints of chaotic lifestyles that reveal that some blacks haven't gotten as far away from the influence of whites as they may think they have. You'll see in their lifestyles a tangled mesh of contradictions and weird behaviors that are as confusing as the sight of bourgeois black kids hanging on a street corner, sucking brew.

A rush of activity flows through the shopping-center parking lot most evenings, when the professional blacks, returning from their oppressive jobs, zip to *this* shop or *that* store to pick up necessities. One by one, you see them rolling in, driving gleaming late-model Lexuses, Benzes, and Jeep Cherokees with disoriented-looking children strapped inside. Although they sport the trappings of prosperity, they don't seem happy. They look hurried and harried, tense—as uptight as the white people they emulate.

Every day, the frantic pattern at that shopping center repeats itself as predictably as the rising of the sun: After collecting their kids from day care and school, many parents stop first at the Blockbuster Video outlet and rent movies to baby-sit their children for the evening. From there, it's on to the McDonald's to pick up Happy Meals. Then, they head home, where the kids wolf down their high-cholesterol food and watch TV while Mama and Daddy collapse upstairs and try to catch their shortening breath.

It's success, white American style. It's blacks blindly caught up in the daily performance of what one writer in *The New Yorker* described as "the adrenaline surge that accompanies perhaps the fiercest desire of all these days—the desire to get ahead."

Although few would admit it, many of the blacks of P.G. County also pattern their lives on whites' lives in other, more subtle ways. When I first moved to the county, the complaint I heard most often was that expensive retailers, such as Macy's, Lord & Taylor, and other high-end businesses that follow white money everywhere had failed to open branches in P.G. I wondered whether those blacks really understood what they were saying: Without being aware of it, they were saying that they were upset that white retailers were refusing to come in and *exploit* them. They seemed to overlook the possibility that white racism could provide motivation for blacks to create their own businesses.

Fortunately, there is a sprinkling of black businesses operating in P.G. Black entrepreneurs recently opened BET SoundStage, an elaborate black-theme restaurant owned by Black Entertainment Television. And soul-food joints are springing up everywhere.

But for the most part, black business development in P.G. has followed the same pattern as it follows in poor neighborhoods: There's a glut of black barbershops and hair salons, and there's a black shopping mall nearby. (You can tell the black malls by the proliferation of stores that sell gold chains, beepers, and Payless shoes.)

Lots of nonblacks certainly have no problem recognizing the business potential in P.G. County. In recent years, as word has spread that there's black money to be had, a rainbow of other races has stormed into the county and set up businesses. There's a Jerry's Pizza place on Central Avenue, but it's not run by anybody named Jerry. It's owned and run by a group from Pakistan, who pooled their resources and bought the franchise. There's a carryout seafood joint, where you can buy crabs by the barrel. The place is named Homeboys, but the owner is white. At Kettering Plaza, there's a place called simply Beauty Barber. There, you can buy all kinds of special products for blacks—much of it adorned with the colors and symbols of African kinte cloth. You can buy nappy Afro wigs and hair products galore that come in tall bottles that say MADE BY AFRICANS FOR AFRICANS. You can also buy products whose labels declare that they are manufactured by companies that are 100 PERCENT AFRICAN AMERICAN OWNED. But the store is run by Koreans.

"The Asians are like fleas on the back of a dog," one resentful friend complained. "You can't get rid of them. They follow black folks around, sucking blood, wherever they go."

There is a determination among the P.G. blacks to demand respect, especially from the foreigners who come to their communities and earn livelihoods off them. The problem is, their commitment to the struggle is often expressed in ways that are uniquely black bourgeois.

Once, they protested when Eddy's, a new Chinese takeout

restaurant in Lake Arbor, refused to provide seats for customers waiting for their orders. The demonstration was cool, but it was hard to get fired up about it after seeing all those well-heeled folks out in front of the place in their monogrammed shirts and expensive suits, marching and waving protest signs.

On another occasion, they protested when the Giant Food store in Kettering Plaza placed magnetic detectors near the doors to catch shoplifters. One irate woman told me, "We wanted to let them know that blacks out *here* don't steal."

I went to the Giant and asked a black employee about the matter. He chuckled as if reflecting on the pretentious head trips that sometimes come with being black and middle-class. The employee told me that store managers put up the detectors after learning that in the previous year, twenty thousand dollars worth of merchandise had walked out the door.

At some point, neighborhood activists who met with the management demanded that the "insulting" detectors be removed, but the management refused. "I guess they lost that battle," the store employee said.

"Yeah," I told him. "That's not the only battle they've lost."

Of course, it's also a status statement among some blacks in P.G. County to imitate white folks' obsession with protecting their property values. When it comes to that property, some blacks proved they can be as racist toward their people as some white folks are. In Perrywood, when too many young black boys and men began gathering at a basketball court, distressed "activists" encouraged the police to get aggressive with them. Just as they have harassed brothers in white areas, the police began randomly confronting young black men at the court, demanding that they show proof that they live in the neighborhood.

And dig this. Blacks in a section of P.G. called Woodmoor, where homes run around five hundred thousand dollars, campaigned successfully to get a new zip code because the old one associated them too closely with a place called Landover, where many lower-income blacks live.

For all the confusion among blacks in P.G. County, there is some cause for hope. Recently, a group of black churches banded together and launched a plan to form their own banks, which would extend loans to black businesses and home buyers, who routinely get turned down by white lenders.

The promise of that and other, similar efforts leads you to believe—or maybe you just *want* to believe—that the professional blacks of P.G. County are going to work things out. Like middle-class black folks everywhere, they *have* to work it out. Nothing less than the future of black America depends on it.

For the moment, though, it looks rough for the home team. It looks confusing, as conflicting as the notion of African Americans giving lip service to the need to support black life, then acting as if they valued their property more than human beings.

This contradiction has been apparent sometimes in the clumsy ways they've handled problems with young people in some P.G. County neighborhoods. In Lake Arbor, when ballplayers got a little rowdy at a playground court, community activists also did the white reactionary thing—they had the basketball rims taken down without providing a gym or some other alternative recreational outlet for the young.

And as for the young bloods who gather sometimes on the corner to shoot the breeze and drink their brew, they've been taken care of, too. They were ordered to take their confusion somewhere else.

WHITE FEAR

8

THE VIBE

Part I. The Problem with Babies

Sometimes the deepest racial lessons come from the most unlikely souls. For instance, babies, the youngest of the youngest among us, are probably the world's finest teachers. They have an uncanny way of tossing out pearls of wisdom that reveal just how shallow we old heads are.

It's true. Where race is concerned, babies are wiser, much wiser, than us witless adults. Take the drama that unfolded one day in Atlanta, at a fast-food place. I'd gone into Long John Silver's and ordered a fish sandwich (with hot sauce) to go. While waiting for the order to be filled, I took a seat on a long cushioned bench up against the wall.

Minutes later, a plump white woman walked in with her

child in tow. She placed her order, then took a seat at the far end of the bench, about ten feet down from where I sat. There was nobody between us.

The woman appeared to be in her early thirties. She had an air of smugness about her, an expression I often see in the Deep South. I've come to think of it as a kind of bitterness that southern whites still harbor about having lost the Civil War.

I guessed her baby was less than two years old. He had thin red hair, blue eyes, and no more than three teeth in his tiny head. He sat safely in his mama's lap awhile; then he campaigned to get down and explore the restaurant.

Once down, he stumbled around unsteadily, drifting a few steps away from his mom. When he'd thoroughly checked out his immediate area, he looked around for new terrain. That's when he spotted me.

The problem with babies, you see, is that race means absolutely nothing to them. They show a kind of passive contempt for the ingrained prejudices their elders embrace; they don't give a whit about the racial boundaries we erect. And so when they're out in public, toddlers can't be trusted to behave in an appropriate way.

That baby at Long John Silver's stared long and hard, as if he were waiting for me to acknowledge him. When I looked his way, he flashed a precious, irresistible smile. I smiled, too, then glanced at his proud mother. When our eyes met, we nodded cordially in the way that grown-ups do when conceding universal love for a baby whose wonder fills a room.

Where babies are concerned, there's an unspoken truce between blacks and whites. In our condescending ignorance, we presume that children's naïveté is what makes them color-blind. We assume they'll learn better in due time. And so when babies have center stage, blacks and whites regard each other more civilly. For the sake of the children, we suspend our animosities and ignore their racial indiscretions as best as we can.

With some effort, the baby's mother and I complied with that unwritten code. But then the toddler did something that threatened to shatter our fragile racial truce: He stumbled clumsily toward me, smiling coyly, indicating, I assumed, that he wanted to play.

Until that moment, it hadn't dawned on me that I might be about to do something that I'd never done before: I'd never played with a white stranger's child. I'd done the *coochie-coochie-coo* routine and frolicked with lots of black kids. It was the most natural thing to do in places like shopping malls and on checkout lines, where people find themselves thrown together in proximity. But my racial defenses had never before permitted me to consider taking such liberties with white children. This child's charm was infectious enough to prompt me to try.

I glanced at the white boy's mother, offering a smile as I looked for tacit permission to play with her son. But she didn't return my smile. Instead, she responded with a grudging, tight-lipped look that, without words, shouted a resounding *no*. I took the woman's deadpan demeanor as ample warning and decided to leave Junior alone.

I have a theory about this sort of thing. I suspect that babies secretly plot to make fun of grown-ups when we behave in childish ways. I think babies deliberately draw black adults and white adults into awkward racial predicaments. Then, they sit back and watch us squirm—maybe that's why babies smile so much.

Pretending to be unaware of the delicate racial dynamics surrounding him, the toddler waddled around across the floor, occasionally stopping at the far end of the bench to flash another one of his patented grins. He seemed oblivious of the few other patrons who entered and left the restaurant, as well as to the servers behind the front counter, who were shouting out orders and handing folks their food. He was completely homed in on me.

Whenever he beamed at me, I'd respond by smiling, too.

Then I'd turn away, hoping to discourage the kid from approaching me. But he wasn't having that. The toddler climbed on the bench, right between me and his nervous mom. Then he climbed back down, repeating the game several times. Each time, he inched closer to where I sat.

I glanced at his mother. By this time, she seemed to be growing more anxious. She wondered, I guessed, what she'd do if her baby enticed me to lift him up.

Full of nervous energy, she shifted uncomfortably in her seat. Then, she fumbled and dropped some papers that she'd been pretending to read. Every time her baby moved toward me, she shifted uneasily again. At one point, she got up and grabbed her son. But he protested. He wriggled and squealed and made such a scene that she eventually turned him loose.

I must admit, I got a little jittery, too. I didn't know what I'd do if the kid touched me. I wondered, *Should I lift him and play with him? Would his mother freak at the sight of black hands touching her child?*

I also began to resent the little blue-eyed bugger for putting me on the spot. At the same time, I felt childish, downright foolish for brooding over such a trivial thing.

It was apparent, though, that this matter couldn't be taken too lightly. Looking at the boy's edgy mother, I sensed the potential for an ugly scene. She gave off an unfriendly vibe. Sitting there in a summer dress with ruffled sleeves, she evoked images of hoopskirts and bonnets, southern crackers and hanging trees.

Looking at her, I was reminded of a scene that had occurred a few months earlier at a Maryland restaurant, where two toddlers generated a lot more racial tension. Two groups—one black, the other white—had sat at tables across from each other. The black group had a little boy, about two years old, with them. The white brood had a girl who appeared to be about the same age as the black toddler.

When the little white girl spotted the black boy, she instinctively sought to play with him. Behaving just like the toddlers they were, they disregarded the social customs that govern our civilized land. Without introductions or any of the silly formalities adults get hung up on, they took to each other right away.

They played peekaboo and hide-and-seek; then the little boy began chasing the girl around the dining room. He chased her nonstop among the tables and chairs, delighting other customers, who watched and laughed. Whenever he caught her, he'd grab her around the waist, pretending to be the bogeyman. The girl would shriek merrily, then dart off again to some other spot.

In time, all this proved to be more than those Caucasians could stand. Literally, it was child's play. But I suspect it symbolized something far more serious for those white adults. I suspect that the sight of a black boy chasing a white girl conjured up age-old stereotypes of black men, white women, and taboo lust.

Without saying a word, the girl's father abruptly rose from his seat, went over, and snatched his laughing daughter from the boy's playful clutch. Then, he turned on his heels and went back to his seat.

Of course, the black boy's parents got defensive. They sat up straight in their chairs. They were trying, I guessed, to figure out whether the white man's action amounted to a racial slight. The other adults at the two tables seemed uptight, too. For a moment, the tensions grew thick and hung heavy in the air as they all sat there, embarrassed and annoyed at the same time. Then, the white folks did a smart thing—they got up and left before hostile words could be exchanged between the two groups.

Somehow, because of one absurd, silent exchange, everybody had a ruined evening—everybody except those two giddy toddlers, who just wanted to have fun.

I thought about that scene as I sat at the Long John Silver's in Atlanta and determined to ignore the childish impulses that had conquered those people in that Maryland restaurant. My resolve was shaken, though, when the affable toddler moved yet closer to me.

I shifted, glanced nervously at my watch, and wondered why it was taking so long to fill my order. Then, my worst fear surfaced. The baby crept even closer and held out his arms, imploring me to lift him up.

My palms grew moist. I looked at his mother, sitting there in her ruffled dress, giving off her ugly vibes. She responded with a glare that seemed to say, *Don't you* dare *touch my child!*

I knew she wanted to snatch her baby up again. But I suspected she was reluctant to make her racial misgivings too obvious to the handful of other blacks and whites who had come in, ordered food, and by now were standing around, intently watching us. Instead of risking a scene, she called to her son in a crisp, Deep South Georgia twang. "Jason, come 'ere. Come on."

Ignoring his mother, little Jason eased even closer to me.

I grew antsy. He had a mischievous look on his face that puzzled me.

His mother called, louder this time, "Jason . . ."

He came closer, to within two feet of me.

The woman called again. She seemed seriously uptight now, almost panic-stricken. I thought the broad was headed for a nervous breakdown.

As Jason moved closer to me, his mother slid to the edge of her seat, poised to bolt forward to intercept him. But she tried to be cool. Unable to coax her child to chill, she tried to lure him back by rattling some fluorescent-colored plastic toy. "Come 'ere, sweetie."

I sweated the whole scene. At that point, the quiet tension between Jason's mother and me was almost more than I could bear.

Jason moved closer, raising his fat fingers toward my knee. I braced myself, half expecting to hear his mother shriek.

But the sound I heard didn't come from her. It came from the front counter, where I'd ordered my grub. "Numbers nineteen and twenty!" The store cashier had called my number. My fish sandwich (with hot sauce) was ready.

Relieved, I jumped up and dashed to the counter, escaping Jason's tiny clutch. In the same instant, the white woman sprang from her seat and met me there—the cashier had called her number, too.

We both got our food and made a break for the door. Along the way, the white woman scooped up Jason and pushed her way through the exit. Like her, I made a beeline for the parking lot.

As his mother carried him off to their pickup truck, Jason looked at me one last time before being placed in his car seat. He waved the tightfisted half wave that babies wave; then he smiled the strangest smile. It wasn't your typical innocent baby's grin. It was more like a knowing smirk—I swear there was a twinge of amused cynicism in that baby's face, a look that seemed to say, *I just had a great time at your silly expense.*

I slid into my car, sat there, and pondered the intricacies of the whole ordeal. The more I thought about it, the more it seemed that two adults had just been played. I'm convinced. That baby held a mirror before his mother's face and mine, then sat back and mocked our racial clumsiness.

That's the problem with babies. They know too much. And they don't give a damn about the racial boundaries that grown-ups impose.

Or maybe the problem with us adults is that we do.

Part II. The Elevator Ride

You bop out of your hotel room, tipping ever so lightly so as not to disrupt the cuffs of your gabardines, which are falling—just right—over your Paolo De Marco shoes.

You punch the elevator button, and while you wait, you glide to the wall mirror for *one* last look before heading out to greet the world. You check yourself out, up and down, and, for the umpteenth time, nod your approval: The beige print tie is slick. The olive sport jacket is coordinated— brilliantly, you think—with the cream-colored slacks.

The elevator light flashes, and you hear the familiar *ting!* letting you know it's time to go.

The door opens. You step inside, set down your briefcase,

and take your place across from a middle-aged woman who looks as if she'd just been spooked. But you're too wrapped up in you to be concerned with her. Your thoughts drift into space, reviewing the details of your business date.

As you ponder, the lighted elevator numbers announce your descent: *12, 11, 10 . . .*

At some point, your concentration snaps. You're being watched. The woman is staring hard enough to make you wonder, *Is there milk or mustard on my coat lapel?*

You feel *the vibe.* It's the same vibe you felt the other day, standing in line behind some twitchy white dude at an ATM.

Now a different set of eyes is fixed on you.

It takes a moment to grasp the tension that's filled the elevator car, choking the air like toxic gas. Then you catch on—it's fear. *White fear.*

Of course, you could be completely wrong. It's possible that this woman's thoughts are a million miles away. It's possible that she hardly noticed you. But this is America, where racial suspicion rules. Here, blacks are expertly trained to interpret white folks' every move.

In predicaments in which blacks and whites find themselves with each other in isolation, strange things happen inside their heads. Deeply ingrained, twisted racial notions govern their thoughts, especially where white women are concerned.

White women are forbidden fruit. According to the myth, you want her. According to the myth, you ache to be near her ivory skin. According to the myth, you yearn to kiss her ruby lips. As the myth goes, you long to caress her tender arms— arms pure as the driven snow.

The woman in the elevator has that *look,* that expression that seems to say she knows the myths. She suspects what you want, and she seems filled with the wildly absurd terror that, in the brief ride between the twelfth and first floors, this *black* man may rape her, rob her, and leave her for dead.

Can't she see from your dress and your demeanor that you obviously have a job? Can't she tell from your bearing that you're no rapist or thief?

It doesn't matter. White fear eludes rationality.

You scrutinize her. She's cross-eyed, knock-kneed, and pigeon-toed. Got teased hair, a flat butt, and crooked teeth. Cellulite is probably massed from waist to knees. You want to burst into laughter. You want to laugh hysterically and ridicule her. You want to jeer and laugh until your belly aches.

But no, this is serious. She's afraid, and fear—white fear— can cost you your life. Ask Emmett Till's mother or the Scottsboro boys what white fear can do. Ask black old-timers in Rosewood, Florida, or in Tulsa, Oklahoma, where a chance encounter between a black man and a white woman—in an elevator just like this—led a town full of rabid whites to launch a lunatic killing binge. Ask blacks up North in Boston, where Charles Stuart, a white man, murdered his pregnant wife and told the police a black man did it; or quiz brothers down South in Union, South Carolina, where a white woman named Susan Smith drowned her two kids, then claimed a black carjacker had kidnapped them.

White fear.

Blacks have much more reason to be afraid of whites than they have to be afraid of us. Black fear gets dismissed, but white fear gets attention. Take the white woman in Florida who filed a lawsuit seeking a disability pension from her employer. Said she was once robbed by a "big, black man." Said she's still traumatized. Said she's unable to work among big, black men.

The woman in the elevator looks, well, traumatized. *But this isn't Florida. This is Virginia.*

On second thought, that could be worse. Virginians just passed a decree allowing "law-abiding" citizens to carry concealed weapons to protect themselves from "criminals."

The racial implications of that law worries you. In the thinly veiled white vernacular, *law-abiding* means "white." In the thinly veiled white vernacular, *criminal* is merely a synonym for "black."

Suppose *this* "law-abiding" woman has a gun. She could

shoot you in a heartbeat—blow you away—and she'd be free on bail by suppertime. She could tell the judge she *thought* you threatened her. Tell him she feared for her life. Tell him she was traumatized—by a *black* man. Automatically, he'd understand.

Suddenly, you don't feel like laughing anymore. Now, you're afraid, as scared of this woman as she is of you. You're also angry, pissed off—at her, at the world, at the way things are. You even get mad at yourself for entertaining foolish fears. You wonder, *Am I being paranoid?*

Quickly, quietly, the reminder comes: *This is America. Paranoia here is justified.*

Finally, the elevator slows and lurches to a halt. Only a few seconds have passed since you first got on, but it feels as if you'd spent an eternity imprisoned there.

The light flashes. The bell sounds, *ting!* The door opens, and you rush out, relieved, delighted to be free again.

9

THE WHITE CHURCH

It's amazing to see that some blacks still look to white folks to lead them to a fabled promised land. Even at this late stage in the ruthless American survival game, some blacks trust with unyielding faith that somebody white will steer them home.

That delusion seems a bit insane, like expecting the fox to save the hens. Foxes don't save hens, and even the most well-meaning, God-fearing whites don't deliver blacks from their problems—be they political, economic, social, or otherwise.

I realized that late one night years ago while riding down a dark and winding road with a friend, a guy we called Itchy Booty. We were returning home from deep in the country, where we'd scored some *monster* reefer from a hillbilly white boy. (We could always depend on the white boys to have the best dope. They were closer to the *real* connections, the international hookups that provide the uncut stuff.)

Itchy Booty and I were both very tired. Not physically. We were emotionally drained. I'd been through a series of hassles recently: a new baby, no job, no money—the usual headaches. Given some of the crazy things I'd been doing on the streets, it was clear that, as they say in the Bible, the end was nigh at hand. It was just a matter of time, and I was racing the clock, trying to stay a step ahead of the gunshot, the OD, or the police bust.

Itchy Booty had his own problems. Plain and simple, he was a dope fiend, the kind of user the tough-talking politicians classify as a criminal. Itchy Booty was no criminal. He was just a supersensitive guy. He was despondent, one of many dudes in my neighborhood who got high all the time because they couldn't face the world's harshness. So they fired up and copped out—every chance they got.

We rode down the highway, testing the new herb we'd scored and thinking to ourselves about the problems we faced. I was nineteen. Itchy Booty was two years older. (His real name was Herman, but we called him Itchy Booty because somebody once caught him scratching the crack of his behind, scratching hard and deep, like the itch actually was *under* his skin.)

To us, at that age, the world, especially the white world, looked strange and intimidating. We were on the threshold of venturing into that world to face the Man. We were big-time scared, and the paralyzing fear, along with the daily string of disappointments piling up, left us downhearted. We were so blue that instead of turning on the radio, we shared our gloom like we shared that joint—in silence.

At some point, Itchy Booty broke the quiet, and we began to rap. We talked about a lot of things—real-life issues that brothers seldom broach unless they're high or deeply depressed or both. We talked about women; we talked about our pain; of course, we talked about white folks; we talked about how hard it is finding work; we even talked about religion.

During the exchange, Itchy Booty looked at me and asked, "Hey, man, you ever go to church?"

I shook my head. "Naw, bro—it's been many, many moons."

We laughed, then grew quiet again, letting the power of the marijuana sink in deep. I hadn't done a lot of thinking about religion before. Ordinarily, that topic would've been taboo, one of those things you didn't discuss for fear it might make you choke. But when you're feeling low, you tend to be more open to that sort of thing. When you're down, you tend to be more receptive. In my depressed state, I'd become receptive. I'd begun to think about God a lot.

I didn't know until then that Itchy Booty had been thinking about God, too. He said a friend had taken him one recent Sunday to a place called Rock Church. He'd gotten down on his knees and prayed, and he came so close to accepting Jesus into his life that it scared him.

"I actually enjoyed it there," he said. "It was kinda strange, but it made me feel better. I felt like I was closer to God, like if I had him on my side, I could get myself together. It made me feel high just being there. It was a different, more natural kind of high. . . . I'm definitely going back to that church, man."

The conversation was getting too mushy. I lightened the mood with an offhand joke. "Well, if church can get me *high,* I'm definitely down for that."

We chuckled, then rode some more in silence. Eventually, we reached a place called Smithfield, a racially mixed Virginia farming community known for its tasty country hams. Riding along a little farther, we came to a church. The lights were on, and cars filled the parking lot. It looked as though a Saturday-night party were going on.

I said, half in jest, "I'll bet them black folks jumpin' in there."

Suddenly, Itchy Booty looked at me and smiled. "Let's go check it out."

At first I thought he was kidding. "You mean go to church? On a Saturday night?"

"Yeah."

When I searched his eyes, it was clear he was as serious as a heart attack. That's what I liked about Itchy Booty. He was always looking for another kind of high, always looking for a bigger, better head trip. But me, I was scared to go inside. For one thing, there was a cemetery right beside the church.

I also was scared because I didn't know what would happen if I went in there. I didn't know how I'd handle it. I'd been to church and seen people—grown people—overcome by something spooky. They called it the Holy Ghost. They'd jumped right up out of their seats, screaming and crying out to "sweet Jesus."

That might've been OK for them, but for me it was too much like losing control. Hanging in the streets, I was trying to be hard. You can't be hard and allow yourself to get so emotional about something that you lose control.

I knew that if I stepped into that church, it was possible I'd lose it like those Holy Rollers. As bad as I felt, I feared that if

I went inside, the weight of all my problems might come tumbling down on me at once and I would break down and cry. I didn't want anything like that to happen to me—definitely not in public. "I dunno, man," I said, shaking my head skeptically.

But Itchy Booty was persistent. "C'mon, man, let's check it out. You might be able to find God."

For some odd reason, I'd been hearing that a lot lately—that I needed to find God. Several old people had told me stuff like "Jesus wants you" and "give yourself to the Lord."

One day in my hometown of Portsmouth, Virginia, I had run into my sixth-grade teacher, Mrs. Odessa Macklin. She was very religious. She'd dropped one of those cartoon Bible pamphlets on me and asked, "Are you saved?"

And I'd asked myself, *Saved from what?* I was polite to my old teacher, but I got away from her the first chance I got. I knew that if the conversation went on much longer, she'd try to lead me to the Lord. She'd offer to help me find God. So I got away—from Mrs. Macklin *and* from the Lord.

Now, here I was being confronted with God, or by God, again. It made me wonder whether maybe God was trying to tell me something. It might've been the reefer talking, but something urged me to let my defenses down. It prodded me to open myself to the possibility that God could salvage what was left of my reckless life.

I knew that going onto God's turf would give him a better chance of rescuing me. And deep inside, I *wanted* to be rescued. Lord knows my heart yearned for something real. I'd spent so much time on the streets being unreal that I was tired, almost too tired to run anymore.

So when Itchy Booty suggested we go inside the church and check out the service, I did something I never would've done ordinarily: I decided to slide into church on the sly and see whether I could *really* get another kind of high. I decided, then and there, to give myself a chance to find God.

No doubt, I was ripe for salvation. By agreeing to walk into a church service, I was reaching out, desperately searching for something spiritual to feed my weary soul. *Maybe, just maybe,* I thought, *this church visit will mark my moment of reckoning.*

We parked the car, got out, and walked slowly toward the door. It seemed like the longest walk I'd ever taken. As we approached the steps that led up to the entrance, I could hear the sound of people singing some church hymn, accompanied by the faint strains of an organ. At the top of the stairs, Itchy Booty reached out and pulled the door latch. When the door opened, the sound of a chorus spilled out into the night air.

We had taken no more than a half step through the doorway when we were met by an usher, who gave us the shock of our tattered lives. He was a *white* man! We'd mistakenly stopped at a white church!

Instantly, when I saw that white man, I lost my high. All that reefer zipped right out of my bloodstream, and I was as sober as a nun in prayer.

The white man appeared to be just as startled as we were. He stared at us, and we stared at him, none of us knowing what to say. For a second, it looked as if he were about to slam the door. But he couldn't. After all, this was a church. The doors of the church are supposed to be open to everyone. The usher was expected to show faith and charity. He had no choice but to invite us in.

When he'd collected himself, he strained to reshape his hellish scowl into a heavenly smile. It didn't quite work. He produced one of those embarrassed, red-faced smiles that whites put on when caught off guard. Then, he said something awkward like, "Well, uh, hi—welcome."

I glanced at Itchy Booty, indicating that I wanted to slide back to the car. He stood there looking unsure of himself. I can't imagine what the usher must have thought. Itchy Booty was a slim-jim like me. He was pitch-black, had big, bulging eyes, a little pea-sized head, and hair that looked like mice titties, each tiny nap standing on its own.

Looking sheepishly at the white man, he said, "We came to worship with y'all."

The man still wavered. Nevertheless, he yielded to his moral obligation. "Come on in."

Itchy Booty gave a grateful smile and nudged me through the door. We passed through the vestibule and took seats in the very last pew. Instantly, a sea of horrified white faces in our row turned to stare at us.

Itchy Booty seemed calm. (He had a white girlfriend. He'd grown used to racial tension.) But I was fidgety. I leaned over to him and whispered, "Let's get the hell outta here, man."

It's true that in my time of need, I wanted to seek the face of God. But at the moment, there was a more urgent matter pressing me: probation. To remain out of jail, I had to stay clean for an entire year. Under the terms of my probation, I wasn't supposed to travel beyond a certain boundary without permission from my probation officer. Smithfield was definitely out of bounds.

The last thing I needed was for those panicked white folks to call the law. If they did, how could I explain to my PO that I'd left my restricted boundaries to go to a *white* church—with a dude named Itchy Booty? And if I told a lawman that I'd come to the church to find God and not to rob those white people, he would've found that hard to believe. Hell, I hardly believed it myself.

I looked around the room. At the front of the church was a large cross, flanked by a huge picture of a white Jesus. I knew very little church history. But seeing that picture reminded me of something an old head once told me. He explained some of the peculiar things white folks do with their Bible and their church. He said that from Billy Graham on down, they interpret the Bible in ways that suit their purposes. He told me that using their verbal hat tricks with "God's word," the white church has remained the bedrock of white supremacy—throughout slavery and segregation and right on up until today. "Whites," he said, "count themselves among the truest believers."

I knew he was right. I'd seen white people who believe deeply that God is on their side; I'd seen whites who believe God is white and biased, just like them. I'd seen them, before heading off to some needless war, pause and pray to God for victory, never considering that God created their opponents, too. I'd seen them, and I knew they believed. Klansmen believe, militiamen believe, right-wing conservatives believe—they couldn't all be so stubbornly racist if they didn't truly believe.

And there I was that night, a black man sitting among *true* believers. . . . I wanted to kick Itchy Booty's ass for bringing me there. At the same time, I was also a little curious. I'd often passed by white churches and wondered what went on inside. It didn't seem as though white people did the same things blacks did in church. Blacks sang with fervor; they cried and had a swinging good time with "the Lawd." As far as I could see, they believed in what was taught in the Bible. They believed in faith, hope, forgiveness.

In fact, I thought they believed *too much*. To me, black people were too forgiving. They turned the other cheek and prayed too often in the hope that if things didn't get better in this life, their adherence to the Word would guarantee a better break on the other side.

So I knew what they did in black churches. But nothing in the behavior of cross-bearing whites told me what they did with their time in the house of God. There was nothing in America's white church that demonstrated that they had the faintest idea what it meant to be spiritual. I thought church-going whites were no less cruel to men than they were to beasts.

Even today, years after that excursion with Itchy Booty, when I think of the white church, I think of its blind spots. I think of those flag-waving Christian conservatives. I think about the murders and bombings at abortion clinics, carried out by people who call themselves pro-life. And I see them doing absolutely nothing to save the afflicted lives that are already on this earth.

Back then, I figured that when white people filed into their churches on Sunday mornings, they never wasted time on prayer. I figured they played bingo or did something else to kill time, then went on home at 1:00 P.M.

I'd gotten a glimpse of high-tech white churches on those TV programs that air during the Sunday-morning gospel hour. I'd seen those white evangelists faking the funk—Pat Boone–looking dudes dressed in plaid suits, white belts, and matching white shoes. Their hair would be slicked back, real greasy, like Elvis Presley's in his prime. When the camera panned the audience, I'd seen thousands upon thousands of whites praising the Lord. Sometimes I'd laughed as I watched, and I'd wondered whether those preachers ever really challenged their flocks.

Sitting in the Smithfield church with Itchy Booty, looking over that congregation, I sensed this pastor hadn't challenged his. It looked like redneck heaven in there. And it was dead as hell. The minister preached in a dull monotone on some topic that escapes my memory. The people sat there, quiet, seemingly unmoved by anything he said. They may as well have gone next door and held the service in the cemetery.

It didn't take long for word to ripple through the congregation that there were two *black* men there. It created a real stir, like a domino effect. People turned their heads, checking us out one by one. Like a wave, the ripple moved toward the front of the room and finally reached the boring preacher. He sensed from the commotion that something was going on, that there was some distraction in God's house. When he caught sight of Itchy Booty and me, a look of pure terror spread across his face. He tried to remain cool. He carried on with his drab sermon, but you could see he was preoccupied.

By then, I'd begun to lose hope of finding God. I struggled to remain receptive, but it was hard. There was no semblance of brotherly love or spiritual warmth flowing my way. There was only suspicion and, I suspected, hatred.

I figured that if those folks could get past our skin color and see our deepest needs, they might be able to find it in their hearts to help lead us to spiritual deliverance. But they were blind, so blind, in fact, that they looked right past our needs. My own suspicions about them may have led me astray on this, but I thought they saw nothing *but* our color.

And the blindest among the flock, it seemed, was the preacher. He fumbled through his words in search of a tasteful way to end his sermon. I knew he ended the sermon early; it seemed he cut off his point right in midthought. There were no closing words to speak of, and he didn't even bother to ask whether anybody wanted to come forward and be saved.

When the reverend said, "Let us all bow our heads for the closing prayer," I don't think a single white person complied. Those congregants weren't about to close their eyes and let their defenses down with two niggers in God's house.

The faithful filed quickly out of church, casting nervous glances at us along the way. After exchanging a weak handshake and an awkward greeting with the spooked pastor, Itchy Booty and I went to our car, all the while being eyed suspiciously by a group of wary white men who had gathered on the side.

Once inside the car, I breathed a deep, long sigh of relief. I was glad to get out of there. At the same time, a kind of sadness washed over me. It seemed that my shot at salvation had frittered away. I'd gone in there looking to find God and left feeling that I'd somehow stopped at the wrong address.

Years later, when I learned more about God, I ran across a Scripture that characterized how I felt about those whites. The Scripture says, *"How can you say you love God, whom you have not seen, when you don't love your fellow man, whom you see every day?"*

Of course, I didn't know at the time that it would be a long while before I'd see the inside of a church again. Shortly after that adventure, life would come crashing down hard on Itchy Booty and me. I would violate my probation and wind up in prison for armed robbery. Itchy Booty would die a slow death, the death of a user who spends his time in drug houses, begging for a free hit.

Before we pulled out of the parking lot, I took one last look at the country church. I somehow knew that I'd learned a very valuable lesson: White America is more in need of spiritual leadership than anybody else, and it will never occur to them that their failure to find salvation is linked to their inability to connect with the humanity in blacks, even in a place of worship.

Itchy Booty and I had gone to that white church as two scared sinners reluctantly delivering themselves to God's color-blind altar with the hope of redemption. In a symbolic way, we'd done what blacks in America have done all along: relied on whites' profession of faith to reel us in. But the sight of two blacks had sent their faith running for cover.

As those people filed from the church, I shook my head at the pitiful sight. And then a voice spoke to me about deliverance. The voice spoke almost as if it had come from on high. It said, *Blacks can't look to white folks to save them. White folks can't even save themselves.*

REDEMPTION

10

MUHAMMAD ALI: WE CLING TO HIM

Almost everybody has a Muhammad Ali story. Ever since he burst onto the national scene more than thirty years ago, he has endeared himself to us like no one else. Everyone knows Ali: In the three decades since he first became known as a cocky, outspoken heavyweight boxing champ, he's transformed himself into a worldwide icon and celebrity goodwill diplomat.

Chances are if you haven't run across him at some airport, prizefight, or charity event, your mother, your brother, or your cousin's friend has encountered Ali somewhere at some point in time.

But more intriguing than his seeming ability to be everywhere at once is the man's staying power, his remarkably sustained imprint on the American psyche. Ali left the ring more than sixteen years ago, yet he remains a heroic fixture, especially in black folks' hearts and minds.

We cling to him and to all he represents: Using his boxing celebrity as a public platform, Ali took bold social stands in the 1960s and '70s that showcased black Americans' struggle for racial justice and symbolized the battle for freedom throughout the world. More than any other athlete in this century, he's transcended his sport. And now he seems to transcend time.

We cling to him because he reminds us—in this cold-hearted, cynical age—that there's still virtue in devoting our lives to causes larger than ourselves.

We cling tightly and, for various reasons, needily.

I had my one and only encounter with Ali sometime in the 1980s. And it was a good thing, too. It was good to run across somebody who inspires idealism because, for blacks, the '80s was a time of serious disenchantment. For many of us, those were the years of the reality check. Those were the years that confirmed, beyond a doubt, the futility of waiting for racial reconciliation. We stood by in frustration as white Americans, caught up in the latest wave of greed and patriotic selfishness, took all the racial lessons of the previous decades and pitched them into the garbage can.

In the '80s, I was in Atlanta, covering city hall for *The Atlanta Journal-Constitution.* I'd started out on the political beat somewhat hopeful about the nation's prospects for social change. But by the middle of the decade, when the Reagan revolution seemed to be winning, what little optimism I'd had evaporated, like water in a flaming frying pan.

One day, while sitting in my tiny second-floor city hall–bureau office, someone rushed into the room with some welcome news. "Muhammad Ali is downstairs! He's coming up to see the mayor!"

I grabbed my notepad and dashed out the door. Just as I entered the hallway, the elevator opened, and there he was, the Greatest. Surrounded by a small entourage, Ali stepped out onto the marble floor. His eyes sparkled when he saw folks pouring from their offices to meet him. People came from everywhere, hitting Ali up for autographs. Awestruck, I hung back from the swarm and just stared at the legend.

Dressed in a dark suit, Ali was the same statuesque, caramel-colored champion I'd seen so many times on TV. He had that familiar boyish grin, the slanted eyes, the prominent cheekbones, and hands that were rather small for a cat who once earned a living knocking men out.

When my turn came to get an autograph, I handed Ali my notepad. He took the pad and pen, glanced at me, and nodded a silent hello. Then he lowered his eyes and concentrated on signing his name.

By then, I knew—everybody knew—that even as Ali stood there indulging us, a savage disease called Parkinson's syndrome was busy gnawing at his nervous system like termites unleashed in a wooden house. The disease had begun to take a visible toll. Once agile and animated, Ali moved with the stiffness of a decrepit old man. Once loud and bodacious, he only muttered muffled noises, pointing a finger toward his mouth, as if half hoping to bring forth some audible words.

It took Ali a full minute to write his name. As he scribbled a slow, deliberate scrawl, his trembling was worse than that of an alcoholic craving a drink. Writing his name was such a chore that I felt embarrassed for him. But he didn't seem ashamed at all. He just focused on the task, and when he'd completed it, he handed me the pad, then patiently went on to sign more autographs.

After he'd signed them all, Ali looked again at the crowd, which had swelled considerably now. Ever the showman, he pulled a handkerchief from his suit pocket and held it high for everyone to see. Amused, we looked on while he performed some magic tricks. When the magic act was done, his handlers led him slowly away. He waved a feeble good-bye before being ushered into the mayor's office for a visit with Andrew Young.

As the crowd dispersed, I took my autographed pad and returned to my secluded cubbyhole. I sat down and stared at the famous name that had been signed with such an unsteady hand. The letters were small and carefully connected, like the scrawl of a third-grader learning cursive script.

I sat there a long while and pondered that brief encounter with Ali and felt a number of emotions. Part of what I felt was racial pride. There also was wonder. But mostly there was sadness, mixed with a tinge of anger. It was a quiet, reverent resentment aimed directly at God. Of all the things God had chosen to do, the one that hurt most was that he silenced the man once known affectionately as the Louisville Lip.

Just exactly what is God trying to tell us here? Surely, I thought, *God must know what heroes like Ali mean to us.*

Heroes are important. In their courage and selflessness, they give us ordinary folks higher standards to aspire to. Heroes are valuable, even the larger-than-life white ones manufactured in Hollywood and portrayed in history books.

A life without heroes is a gloomy life, and in the last decade or so that's what the lives of many blacks have shaped up to be. In the '80s, we really began to feel the burden of the void created by the scarcity of folk heroes within our ranks. The '90s are no better. Malcolm, Martin, and Medgar have been dead three decades now, and Arthur Ashe left us several years ago. Among the handful of true idols left, there is Ali, reduced to a fragment of the spirited gladiator he used to be.

What made Ali different from so many other superstars was that the more his stature grew, the more accessible he became to common folks. Tiger Woods may be the new sports sensation, but we won't likely spot Woods walking through our neighborhood. Ali had a knack for popping up in the lowliest of places—a black community here, a pool hall or college campus there. Unbashful about his love for black people, he'd stick around awhile wherever he visited and joke with fans, hug people, and playfully spar with onlookers, pretending to be a shell-shocked boxer having ring flashbacks that might drive him to knock you out. He connected with people on a visceral level that made them feel that their lives, however ordinary, had been touched by someone special.

We cling to him because he was both regular guy and extraordinary man. We cling because he's the one and only of his kind that we have left, and we're intent on savoring him while he's still around.

When I look back over Ali's career, it's as if I've been with him in spirit from the very start. Although I was too young in 1964 to comprehend the significance of the Liston-Clay fight, I sensed from the excitement of the grown-ups around me that something important had happened when he took the heavyweight title from Sonny Liston, who was considered invincible.

I was a young Ali fan way back when the boxer wore his daddy's name—Cassius Marcellus Clay, Jr. Was also there when he joined the Nation of Islam and publicly renounced his "slave" name in the face of American whites' bitter resentment.

And I cheered in '67, when he bucked white folks and refused to go to war in Vietnam. He refused to be silent on that issue when other leaders were scared to speak out. "I ain't got no quarrel with those Vietcong, anyway. They never called me nigger."

It's so common now to romanticize the '60s, but, really, those weren't romantic times. During those times, the system—the white folks who run this show—was quick to punish blacks who stepped out of line. The '60s establishment's reaction to Ali could serve as a case study of America's standard response to blacks who take outspoken social stands: To pressure him to go to war, the government barred him from leaving the country; private-sector whites tampered with his livelihood, suspending his boxing license so he couldn't earn money in the ring; even esteemed "objective" publications, such as *The New York Times,* joined the white public's clamor for Ali's head—in a front-page article that reflected the thinking of many whites, *Times* sports columnist Arthur Daley described Ali as "a mixed-up man" and questioned whether he had the intelligence to think for himself. "If there was skepticism about the sincerity of his motives when he first fell under the sway of the Black Muslims, it exists no longer," Daley wrote. "He has been so thoroughly brainwashed that he now believes what he says, even if the words are put into his mouth by the Muslims."

Even whites within the ranks of the sleazy boxing world got self-righteous about the thing. In 1967, *The Ring* magazine, considered the bible of boxing, refused to grant Ali its prestigious Fighter of the Year award even though its editors acknowledged that he deserved it. A statement in the magazine said his affiliation with the Muslims and his refusal to go to war had a bad effect on the image of boxing: "Most emphatically is Cassius Clay of Louisville, Ky., not to be held up as an example to the youngsters of the United States."

Although Ali never was held up by the status quo as a role model during that time, the "youngsters of the United States" were obliged to think for themselves. Young blacks—and even some young whites—gravitated to him like hogs to slop.

Whenever he fought, the boys I hung out with would show up at our corner the next day and spar for hours on end. Some guys got knocked out cold trying to emulate the Ali shuffle. Other dudes got jock-slapped trying to "float like a butterfly, sting like a bee."

My buddies and I dug Ali as much for his radical politics as for his fighting skills. When I became a teenager, he was the inspiration for my tossing my draft-registration card into the trash.

Ali was far from perfect—the string of shaky business investments and failed marriages throughout the years attests to that. But we dug him because we sensed in him something genuine, the kind of courage and character that folk singers and poets muse about. His lightning speed and boxing skills were amazing, but what was really awesome was that he jeopardized everything in an age when most celebrities take only calculated risks.

A cartoon I saw somewhere perfectly symbolizes the current American creed. The cartoon features several plump white men in pin-striped suits, lounging in a country club, puffing fat cigars and discussing business deals. One man is telling the others matter-of-factly, "I just sold my soul for a fraction of what the damned things are going for." That one sentence could serve as the anthem for the '90s, when politicians routinely auction their souls for votes and millionaire athletes don't dare take public stands that might jeopardize potential endorsement deals.

That's why we cling to Ali—because he stands as a symbol of heroism in these times, which are not heroic at all; because we know that, infirmities aside, his soul has never been for sale.

It's impossible to talk about boxing and Muhammad Ali without talking about race and America. Where race is concerned, boxing is the most candid competition there is. It's an open acknowledgment of what's *really* going on here between this country's blacks and whites. (That comes through clearly when white boxing promoters put up millions of dollars to foster mediocre "great white hopes.")

When Ali fought after 1970, the year he made his long-awaited comeback to the ring, there was always the sense that much more was at stake than the outcome of a boxing match. For blacks of my generation, an Ali fight produced the kind of excitement the old-timers must have felt when Joe Louis rumbled. Whenever Ali climbed into the ring, we knew that he proudly carried the banner for the entire race. And we also knew that most whites rooted lustily for the other guy.

Even in a match between Ali and a black opponent, there was always the feeling that the other guy was *really* white; or worse, he was dismissed as a stooge, an Uncle Tom, sent to knock our hero down.

In 1971, when Ali fought "Smokin' " Joe Frazier, William Mack of *Sports Illustrated* said "it was widely viewed as the greatest single sporting event of this half century." That was before pay-per-view and HBO, so we were forced to tune in to the radio. In actuality, that match was a long-awaited contest between two of the greatest heavyweights in modern times. But I regarded it as something much more sinister: In my mind, the fight was no less than a racial war, a refereed battle between good and evil. I sat there, glued to that box, listening to every round as if the fate of black America rested on the outcome. In the end, when Frazier won, I surprised myself with a response that revealed just how much emotion I'd invested in Ali: Tears rolled down my cheeks.

I've never again seen Ali in person since the day he came to the Atlanta City Hall, but a few years later I discovered for myself just how big a heart he has. A good friend of mine, a convicted armed robber named Mike, took up boxing during a prison stint. When he got out, he enjoyed some success on the local boxing scene in Virginia before making a bid for the big time.

On a whim, he flew to Pennsylvania. When he reached the mountains of Deer Lake, where Ali had his training camp, Mike learned that the champ was out of town. Ali's assistants told him there was no work there for him. So Mike left the camp on foot and hitchhiked as far as he could down the lonely mountainside. Tired and dejected, he sat down on the side of the road and buried his face in his hands. Some time later, a limo drove by, stopped, and backed up. Out stepped Muhammad Ali. "He saw me sitting there with my bags," Mike told me. "He said, 'Say, man, what's wrong?' I told him why I had come there, and he said, 'Let's go sit down and talk about it.' Later, he gave me a job."

Mike's own career never took off, but as a sparring partner he helped Ali train for several fights. He was there during the final days of Ali's career.

There were many spiteful white folks who wanted to see Ali destroyed—in or out of the ring—but they never got that wish. He lost a few fights, but he was set back mostly by something else: himself. He fell victim to the notorious boxer's ego, a stubborn refusal to yield to Father Time; he was set back by an addiction to the bright lights, the center stage, and the roaring crowd. It was the same condition that compelled Sugar Ray Leonard to come out of retirement too many times—the same irresistible drive to fight one more round when there's nothing left to prove.

Now Ali has to pay the ultimate price.

Who would have thought it? Once so animated, now he can barely move; once the brash young dude who "whupped" everybody put before him, he's now being

TKO'd by an illness that no amount of jabs or uppercuts can counteract.

Seeing Ali in his present state rattles many folks, especially black people such as Mickey Russell, a friend of mine who ran across him in a Chicago airport. "I had heard about his illness, but to see him in a nearly vegetable state—it hurt. His wife said he was having a bad day, so I didn't bother him like some other folks did. I just stood there and gazed at him. I was happy that I was able to see him, but for about a week after that, it messed me up. I told everybody I knew how bad I felt—I had always pictured him as being larger than life."

I suppose Ali weeps sometimes when he's off alone watching old fight films and recalling the glory days, the time when he had everything, including his health. But I also suppose he won't allow us to feel sorry for him.

And maybe we shouldn't. Maybe in some incomprehensible, divine way, Ali has gotten what he sought in life. Always a deeply spiritual man, he has seemed to be searching constantly for his sacred mission. And perhaps that calling has been defined now by the loss of his health.

How can that be?

Even as the question is raised, the explanation is clear: Ali is, literally and figuratively, a fighter. He's learned that victory is about perseverance. His head has been jarred by too many Rope-A-Dopes, yet he still fights through "bad" days, traveling the world, spreading goodwill. His efforts to speak are often lost somewhere in the chambers of his battered brain, but he makes a powerful statement without uttering a single word: All Muhammad Ali has to do is show up somewhere—anywhere—and his mere presence speaks reams about heroism and the strength of the human spirit.

Such tenacity seems even to have softened some white Americans' animosity now. The cynic in me suspects it's easier for whites to accept Ali now that he's a silent symbol and no longer a loudmouthed gadfly challenging them to mend their racist ways. But a friend recently offered a view that suggests the motivation may come from somewhere else: "The way Americans look at people is if you take a stand, they may not agree with you, but they respect you for sticking to your principles. . . . Maybe more people understood, as the years went by, that he was correct in that stand."

Maybe some whites *have* finally made peace with what Ali represents. Maybe his life has shown them this: It's entirely possible for a black man to love his country and, at the same time, hate the needless suffering his countrymen put him through.

I've long since lost the piece of paper with Ali's autograph scribbled on it in his unsteady hand. So I rely on the memory of that one encounter, as well as on countless other images that have come to me from grainy boxing reruns and other television clips over the years.

Whenever I see shots of him looking feeble, I flash back to some glorious time long ago, when he was in his splendid prime. I can see Ali now, shouting playfully in Howard Cosell's reddened face; I can see him combing his hair, primping for the cameras during some postfight interview, declaring, "Ain't I pretty?"; I can see him yelling into the news microphones after outpointing Leon Spinks, making history as the three-time heavyweight champion of the world: "I shocked the woorrrld! I'm the greatest! The greatest of allll tiiiiiiiime!"

But the image I'll cherish most is one that recently came across the tube from Atlanta: Ali taking part in the flame-lighting ceremony for the 1996 Olympics. Ali—once called a traitor because he refused to serve America in a war that politicians now admit was wrong—now representing the United States before the world.

It was a moment filled with all the suspense of a championship match. Carrying the flickering torch, Ali's hands trembled like crazy. He walked slowly, as though battling the disease's attempt to spoil the hour. And watching, you feared he might not make it. But Ali being Ali, he prevailed. On an obviously bad day, he beat back Parkinson's as if it were George Foreman trying to knock him out. He lit that flame. Then, with all the world watching, he paused for a long moment, and I saw him just the way I always have: triumphant, his soul intact, standing tall.

11

ON REDEMPTION

The death of family members or friends is always a bummer. It's so depressing you sometimes forget that death may have meaning and purpose. In nature, death nourishes life, and in human, flesh-and-blood matters, death offers enriching lessons—and sometimes healing—for the living.

My homeboy died the other day. At his funeral, I picked up a lesson that unburdened my soul. It was a lesson about the power of forgiveness. The lesson was remarkable, mostly because my running partner—a battle-weary old street hood called Shane—was an unlikely source of inspiration for such a lofty theme.

Shane was a fellow gangbanger from back in the day. Like

most of us who grew up on the block in Portsmouth, Virginia, he had no use for forgiveness. Our credo was rooted in violence, retaliation. We believed, with all the fervor of the saved and the sanctified, that if somebody wronged you, then you were obligated to respond with *twice* the force.

As a member of our crew, Shane did his part to promote that motto. He didn't start trouble, but he was one *helluva* finisher. He got into more scraps than a junkyard dog. There was the time his front teeth got knocked out in a brawl at school. And the time he KO'd Shalo Belly, an old head who'd underestimated the size of Shane's heart. And the time he got jumped at Nick's pool parlor downtown and returned with a shotgun and cleared out the place.

Yeah, Shane believed firmly in the Old Testament prescription of an eye for an eye. So it came as no big surprise several years ago when I heard that he'd killed a man. I don't know what the police reports say, but the word on the street was that Shane acted in response to something that was done to him. According to the street wires, some dudes had sold Shane some bad drugs down in the Jeffry Wilson housing projects, a place so violent that it's commonly called Little Vietnam. When he returned for a refund, the dudes refused to oblige.

Shane couldn't let that slide. Based on street logic, he *had* to strike back. As the thinking goes, acquiescence is a sign of weakness. To forgive such an affront ensures that another offense will soon follow. If word got out that he was easy prey, Shane would've gotten ripped off more than tithers in a storefront church.

And besides, it was a matter of principle. It may seem strange, but principle holds a prominent place in the streets. That's just one of the many perverse contradictions that govern the block. In a heartbeat, thieves, druggies, and two-bit pimps, people who seem totally devoid of integrity, protect their petty principles to the death. I've seen dudes get teeth kicked out over a dime bet in a crap game, and often the violence is justified by a dismissive shrug, like this popular street-corner slogan: "A nigga's gotta do what a nigga's gotta do. It's principle."

As the story goes, Shane left the scene of the drug conflict and returned with a gun. When he spotted one of the dudes sitting in a car talking, Shane stole him. He sneaked up on the guy and caught him completely off guard. In a flash, it was over. After a brief exchange between the two, Shane delivered five quick, efficient shots to the head at point-blank range.

Police launched a manhunt and brought Shane in. He went to trial and was sentenced to life in prison. In a letter that he wrote to me from the joint, he reasoned that he had had no choice. After all, it was a matter of principle. "I did what I had to do," he said.

It made me sad to think that my stickman might never see the light of day again. I also wondered whether he'd ever be freed from the burden of knowing that he'd killed a man. At the same time, I think we both understood his fate. His prison term was the price he paid for handing his destiny over to the laws of the streets.

Shane served his time at a remote dungeon called Augusta Prison, located near Harrisonburg, Virginia. There, he worked in the kitchen and lifted weights. Then one day in the fall of 1996, about seven years into his prison bid, he just up and died. "It was a massive coronary," his younger brother explained. "They said he was dead before he hit the ground."

I suspect that for preachers the funerals of church acolytes and choirboys are easiest to work. But Shane was no choirboy. Putting away a rogue can be a touchy thing. When it's obvious that the dearly departed wasn't so dear, preachers are *really* forced to earn their due. Their job is to somehow put into perspective a wayward life that was seemingly conducted without purpose or form. The trick is to eulogize the dead rascal with dignity and, at the same time, avoid promoting an outright lie.

Anybody who knew Shane understood why his funeral presented a formidable test. For some of the people who crowded into the New Testament Baptist Church in Portsmouth, that was the draw: to check out how you eulogize a dude who lived with a steel plate implanted in his head as a result of a jailhouse scrap; to see whether someone would preach redemption for a guy who died while serving time for a murder rap.

"I knew people didn't know what to think," Dwayne Brashear, Shane's younger brother, told me later. "I think they wanted to hear what could be said about this guy."

It would have been hard for the best of preachers to explain, and give meaning to, Shane's troubled life, and the elderly man who presided over the funeral was not among the best. He must have known it; he didn't even try. After spending the first few minutes of his eulogy groping for a message that just wasn't there, he did what preachers and politicians often do: He skirted the challenge altogether. Rather than take the risk of stumbling over his words, that preacher simply didn't mention Shane at all. Instead, he pulled up from memory a worn-out message that his flock probably knew by heart. He preached a long and fiery sermon—on faith—as if he were addressing a regular Sunday-morning service.

But this was Monday, the preacher's day off, and it was obvious that he didn't intend to work that hard. As he rattled off his tired, Baptist clichés, people looked at him confused. They wondered, as I did, how his message related to the matter at hand, the matter of the violent life and sudden death of Shane.

I didn't expect the reverend to preach Shane into heaven. And I certainly didn't want to hear my main man condemned to hell. I wanted to know whether the divine forgiveness that church folks talk so much about was also available to devoted, lifelong sinners such as Shane. What I needed to hear was a message of redemption.

But the preacher didn't strike that point; maybe he didn't have as much faith as he thought he had.

At one moment, when he noticed that his faith sermon was failing to rouse or even divert the people in the church, the preacher seemed to grow frustrated. "You are a hard bunch to preach to," he said bluntly. Then he sat in his chair, where he should have been all along.

Next up was Shane's little brother, who gave it a more gallant try. Through teary eyes, Dwayne recalled Shane's sense of humor and told us stories about his brother that made us laugh. He said that Shane was no angel by any stretch but added that his brother was no devil, either. Mostly, he explained, Shane was confused about his purpose in life. And he often acted out in anger, in an expression of that confusion.

As Dwayne spoke, I glanced at his sobbing family seated across the aisle and recalled the ordeals Shane had taken them through. There was his rugged father, who more than once was forced to body-slam his rebellious son. And farther down on the pew, seated between Dwayne's other brother, Phillip, and Shane's fourteen-year-old son, was their gray-haired, weary mother. She had repeatedly tried to get him to accept Jesus before he died.

Shane accepted Jesus all right—as only Shane could. Once when he was at home alone loading a sawed-off shotgun, it accidentally fired, blasting a hole through the living room wall. Panicked, he placed a huge picture—of a white Jesus—in front of the hole to conceal it. Shane got busted, though. When his mother returned home, she knew her picture didn't belong in that room.

"Shane lived a very hard life," Dwayne told the gathering. "By watching my brother, I learned about a lot of things that I should do. I also learned a lot about things that I should *not* do."

When he finished, Dwayne sat down, uncertain, I think, of whether he'd effectively verbalized all that he'd wanted to. Then, there was a long pause, a discomforting silence, as folks waited to see if anybody else would take a shot at pinpointing redeeming qualities in Shane's raucous life.

I sat there waiting, too, all the while staring at Shane's open coffin. It was a smoky-gray number trimmed in gold, and it stood less than five feet away.

I felt obligated to say *something* in my partner's behalf. I was compelled to try to convey the complexity of Shane, to paint his life in a light that would help people see his very human side.

I'd faced the same challenge—and fear—years earlier, when Shane went to trial on the murder beef. I'd wanted to offer myself as a character witness. I had never doubted that Shane killed that man. At the same time, I believed with all my heart something that many people seem unable to comprehend: that it's entirely possible for folks who are basically good at heart to do bad things. Shane was caught up, completely, in the streets, but he wasn't a bad person.

But I hadn't been able to force myself to go to the trial. I knew what I'd be up against. I was sure that I'd face a cynical jury that reflected the popular belief that we are mostly the sum of our actions.

Of course, it's easiest to measure a life by simply tallying outward deeds, and sometimes that's close to an accurate measurement. For someone like Shane, I believe, it's more complicated than that. That's not to say that people shouldn't be punished for committing crimes. Without punishment, there would be anarchy. But folks shouldn't be judged entirely on the basis of one or a few impulsive acts. Such a shallow measuring stick fails to make allowance for what's inside.

On paper, the lives of men and women are rarely reflected accurately. We all know of people—businessmen, national leaders—who are rotten to the core, yet their prominent status and their empty service on community boards and in civic groups give them an image on paper that would seem to make them a cinch for heaven's pearly gates.

Shane looked bad—*really* bad—on paper. After all, he'd been kicked out of the military. He'd served time for possession of stolen goods, assault, and attempted arson. He'd killed a man in cold blood. On paper, it would seem that he should go straight to hell.

Shane was always a little bit wild. Once, in junior high school, he pulled the fire alarm on a dare, and we all stood around and watched as bright-red engines sped to the scene. Another time, in a giddy fit of glee, Shane climbed atop a car and leaped from one hood to the next, down a row of parked cars.

On the block, people often mistook his impulsive, light-hearted manner to mean that Shane was a pushover, too. "He was a gregarious guy," Dwayne said. "He was a thrill seeker. He always wanted to joke and laugh and have a good time, but it would always take a wrong turn."

I remembered that Shane was pretty smart in school. And

he had a good upbringing—he was respectful of adults. But the neighborhood where we grew up, Cavalier Manor, was filled with young brothers who were pressured to live up to a macho legacy handed down from older hoods. We strived hard to be like them. Some young people are able to resist the lure of the streets, but Shane and I and our group of fellas couldn't. In our own way, we were weak, and all of us paid a price—in drug stupors, in prison stints, and sometimes with our lives.

What would have happened if I'd tried to talk about all this during Shane's murder trial? I'll never know because I didn't go. And when I think about how Shane acted in court, probably no character witness could have made a difference anyway. But in not going, I felt I'd somehow failed him—and myself.

Shane's funeral represented a final chance for me to redeem myself, to stand up in behalf of my fallen friend—and other black men like him whose names I didn't know.

As the silence in the church grew, I wanted to get up and speak my piece, but my legs wouldn't let me. I sat there in the front row with the other pallbearers, glued to the pew, horrified. Then, in an act of sheer will, I rose and bounded up to the microphone.

As my eyes watered and my voice quaked, I shared a few

thoughts about my longtime friend. I recalled that contrary to outer appearances, Shane was a man of—well—principle. He had a strong sense of integrity—in a street kind of way.

But there was so much more that I didn't share. For instance, those people who didn't know Shane intimately would have no idea that he was generous to a fault. And even fewer folks would believe that although his actions suggested otherwise, Shane was driven largely by deep-seated fear— fear of not being accepted, fear of being taken advantage of.

I certainly didn't tell them how Shane had stood with me once when I was jumped by some guys and severely beaten. We were up against a rival gang, and the dudes in my group had vowed that we would all stand together. When they realized we were outnumbered, they all ran off. But Shane stood right there and made sure our rivals didn't kill me.

It occurred to me while talking in the church that that story was a street anecdote, and it seemed crazy to use an example of violence to make a point about someone's character.

Finally, frustrated because I didn't quite know what else to say, I resorted to my own version of that old preacher's avoidance thing. Instead of launching into a sermon like his, I shared with the church gathering a strange coincidence.

It happened that on November 12, 1996, I was visiting James Madison University and learned that Augusta Prison was located nearby. I decided to go there the next day and surprise Shane with a visit. But the next morning, I couldn't find anyone who knew the way there. And because I was tired from traveling, I talked myself into driving on home. It was on the following day that I learned that Shane had died—on the very day that I would have visited him.

Regret and guilt weighed so heavily on me that I choked up and grew quiet after sharing the story in church. Finally, I stepped down from the podium, feeling defeated again. I'd still failed to explain my friend's tortured life.

Strangely, the most complete assessment of Shane's life came from someone who had never even known him. I met her at his funeral.

Following the service, everybody stood outside in the chilly November air and chatted, like guests at a neighborhood re-union. I exchanged greetings with a bunch of elderly ladies from the neighborhood. Then, one woman approached whom I hadn't seen before. She asked me, "Do you know who I am?"

I said, "No. What street did you live on?"

She said, "I didn't live in Cavalier Manor. I'm Darryl Taylor's mother."

Confused, I said, "Darryl Taylor? I don't know a Darryl Taylor."

Then the woman, whose name was Vessie, said, "Darryl Taylor is the young man that Shane killed."

I was stunned, dizzy. I wanted to ask Vessie Taylor to repeat what she'd said, but I knew that she knew that I'd heard her correctly. So I just stared.

To tell the truth, I'd given little thought to Shane's victim before that moment. I had no idea how many folks had cried over his loss, no clue as to how many other lives he'd touched. I'd never even learned his name.

It's not that I placed no value on this man's life. It's just that since I didn't know him, Shane's victim was a blur to me, a detail that held little more meaning than other minute details of the case—particulars about the crime scene or the size and type of gun used to carry out the hit.

Now there I was, face-to-face with the victim's flesh and blood. Suddenly, Darryl Taylor was *very* real to me. He was as real as my stick partner's still, cold body lying in that casket, waiting to be transferred to its final resting place.

I looked into Vessie Taylor's eyes and wondered why on earth she'd attend the funeral of her son's killer. The first, most logical explanation, of course, was that she was there for revenge. I assumed she'd come to celebrate a kind of poetic justice: She'd lived to witness the murderer meet the same fate that had befallen her son several years before; she'd survived this world long enough to see her son's murderer put away for good. Also, I suspected Ms. Taylor intended to curse me for saying good things about the man who had done something so unspeakably bad to her son.

But then she revealed that her head—and her heart—were in a completely different place. "I came here to pay my respects. I have forgiven Shane for what he did."

Initially, I didn't understand. *Forgiven him?* This was a person who had every right to damn Shane's soul. *Forgiven him?* Hadn't she gone to the trial? Hadn't she heard the details of her son's gory death? And hadn't she seen Shane's behavior in court? During the trial, Shane, still in a retaliation mode, had shown a complete disregard for his actions and for her twenty-nine-year-old son's life. He'd stepped into court that day talking trash and wearing yellow shorts and a red T-shirt emblazoned with the words SHIT HAPPENS.

Despite all that, Ms. Taylor stood before me and unflinchingly insisted she'd forgiven him.

Sensing my confusion, she explained. "I know that I *have* to forgive him. I'm a Christian, and if I can't forgive someone who has done something against me or mine, then I can't expect God to forgive me for what I do to someone else."

I looked deep into her gleaming eyes and felt her sincerity. There was no sign of malice. No hint of revenge. There was a definite look of resolve, of peace, and of pain.

Although Ms. Taylor was a stranger before that moment, I felt as if I'd known her all my life. I saw her as the embodiment of the countless blacks I've seen for countless years—churchgoing, Bible-toting folks whose unflagging belief in redemption reflects a humanity so profound that most of us have no frame of reference for it. These are people who reach down deep into their hearts and dare to believe—really believe—in the Scriptures that have nurtured them.

More than any other people I've seen, black folks believe in redemption. That kind of belief enabled blacks in Alabama to forgive—and then vote for—George Wallace, once an avowed racist who had devoted much of his political career to promoting their misery.

More recently, that same belief enabled blacks in D.C. to forgive Marion Barry, a crack-smoking politician, for publicly lying about his drug addiction. Blacks forgave him, then reelected him to serve another term as mayor, while vengeful whites clamored for Barry's head.

It's ironic that in America, whites—who have committed so many unspeakable wrongs against so many others—can be the most unforgiving people of all. There is, I believe, a dangerous arrogance in people who choose not to forgive.

I don't know what, if any, wrongs Ms. Taylor had committed in her life, but it was clear to me that she, too, believed that she needed forgiveness. She seemed convinced that she couldn't receive divine mercy until she earned it. And what better way to earn it than by extending mercy to someone else?

I also suspect that for Ms. Taylor, a sixty-six-year-old grandmother who's known tragedy for much of her life, forgiveness represented a kind of freedom. She didn't want to live her life encumbered by hate. In a conversation sometime later, she told me that although she had "resented the way Shane acted and showed no remorse in court," she'd decided to give up those feelings of resentment for her own sake. "If you don't forgive, you carry around that little dark thing in your heart, and it pulls you down. I don't need anything to pull me down."

More than that, she seemed to understand that just as no one is completely good, nobody is totally bad. So it was with Shane.

In her understanding, she did what that preacher could not do, and what Dwayne and I fell short of doing. Even though she'd seen only the worst in Shane, she allowed for the unseen goodness in his heart.

Although she couldn't have known it, Vessie Taylor helped me understand why it had been so important for me to explain Shane's life. It was essential because doing so helped me explain my own. I knew Shane so well because I saw myself in him. And if he was in need of forgiveness, then so was I.

Like him, I'd lived a messed-up life. In the years since then, I've been hard-pressed to understand why Shane's destiny took him down a more painful road while I was given another chance at life. The secular folks call it luck. The church folks call it grace—"There but for the grace of God go I."

Darryl Taylor's mother helped me see that maybe on some level I'd already been forgiven. At the funeral service, I reached out and hugged her and told her, "You're a very strong person."

After a moment, we exchanged good-byes and walked away. I took a few steps, turned around, and called back to her, "Ms. Taylor!"

When she returned, I reached out and said, "Let me hug you again. You're special."

I was grateful. Grateful to learn that there was redemption for my homeboy after all. And thankful to know that that meant there is also forgiveness for me.

ACKNOWLEDGMENTS

I would like to extend my deepest thanks and appreciation to the following people who helped, in ways small and large, to make this book happen: Leon Carter; Kim Dailey; Jeff "The Doctor" Frank; Deb Heard; Ann Godoff; Paula Gomes; Karen Williams-Gooden; Monroe Miller, my son; Courtland Milloy; Lillian Patterson; Sharon Shahid; Kay Shaw; Barbara Vance.

INDEX

ABOUT THE AUTHOR

Nathan McCall's autobiography, *Makes Me Wanna Holler,* was a *New York Times* best-seller. The book also won the Blackboard Book of the Year Award for 1995. McCall has worked as a journalist for *The Atlanta Journal-Constitution* and the *Virginia Pilot-Ledger Star*. He is currently on leave from *The Washington Post*. McCall lives in Maryland, just outside Washington, D.C.

ABOUT THE TYPE

This book was set in Sabon, a typeface designed by the well-known German typographer Jan Tschichold (1902–74). Sabon's design is based upon the original letter forms of Claude Garamond and was created specifically to be used for three sources: foundry type for hand composition, Linotype, and Monotype. Tschichold named his typeface for the famous Frankfurt typefounder Jacques Sabon, who died in 1580.